M000300360

FERNS

A Comprehensive Guide to Growing Ferns

for the Home Gardener

GILLEAN DUNK

Angus&Robertson
An imprint of HarperCollins*Publishers*

An Angus & Robertson Publication

Angus&Robertson, an imprint of
HarperCollins*Publishers*
25 Ryde Road, Pymble, Sydney NSW 2073, Australia
31 View Road, Glenfield, Auckland 10, New Zealand

First published in Australia in 1982 under the title of
Ferns for the Home and Garden
This revised edition published in 1994

Copyright © Gillean Dunk 1982, 1994

This book is copyright.
Apart from any fair dealing for the purposes of private study,
research, criticism or review, as permitted under the Copyright Act,
no part may be reproduced by any process without written
permission. Inquiries should be addressed to the publishers.

National Library of Australia
Cataloguing-in-Publication data:

Dunk, Gillean.
 Ferns.

 Bibliography.
 Includes index.
 ISBN 0 207 17971 9.

 1. Ferns, Ornamental. I. Dunk, Gillean. Ferns for the home and garden.
 II. Title. III. Title: Ferns for the home and garden.

635.9373

Cover photograph by Ivy Hansen
Printed in Hong Kong

9 8 7 6 5 4 3 2 1
97 96 95 94

For Graham Farrant, with my gratitude.

CONTENTS

Acknowledgments

I received a great deal of help with the research and writing of both the original edition and this, the second edition, of *Ferns* and I am very grateful to the following people who so generously gave me that help. They are, first and foremost, my valued and erudite friend, Joseph Holland, without whom the task of rewriting would not have been as pleasurable nor as enlightening; Chris Goudey of Lara, in Victoria, who is one of the world's authorities on ferns; Gordon Ling, who made his collection of Victorian period books on ferns available to me and from which many of the illustrations have been taken; Thomas Hazell; Patrice O'Shea; Gael Shannon; Arianthe Galani; Peter Hind of the Royal Botanic Gardens, Sydney — another respected fern specialist; John and Judy Marley of Marley's Fern Nursery at Mt Ku-ring-gai, New South Wales (most of the ferns pictured in the chapter on container-growing are from this nursery); Steve and Cheryl Atkinson; Delys Anderson; Margaret and Stephen Gillespie, who provided both support and encouragement; and Mary White, palaeobotanist, who kindly made available the photographs of fossils taken by Jim Frazier and published in her important and beautiful book, *The Greening of Gondwana* (Reed, 1993).

I am also very grateful to the following photographers, whose skill with light and lens brought the words to life: John Squire of Sorrento, Victoria; Ivy Hansen of Sydney, New South Wales; and George Greblo of Bendigo, Victoria.

And I am especially proud of my daughter, Sarah Forshaw, the illustrator responsible for the lovely botanical colour drawings.

Many of the photographs of individual species of ferns were taken in the fernery and glasshouses of the Royal Botanic Gardens, Sydney; and in the fernery in the grounds of Ripponlea, in Victoria. The administrators of both gardens were very helpful to me in obtaining the photographs and I am grateful to them. Both gardens hold extensive fern collections and are open to the public.

Preface

In 1982, when the first edition of this book was published, it filled a gap in the existing fern literature, between the detailed works of botanists and collectors, and the all-too-often sketchy and inaccurate instructions in general gardening books and popular gardening magazines — a gap where the needs of the gardener wishing to cultivate ferns for pleasure and interest were not met. To my knowledge, after more than ten years, that gap has remained unfilled by any other works, and this new edition of *Ferns* will, I am confident, maintain its important place; and maintain it in an authoritative and pleasing way.

The original text has been largely rewritten to include the latest scientific and practical knowledge about growing these lovely plants; the list of ferns in Chapter 8 has been expanded to include new varieties now being cultivated; and any changes to botanical or popular names have been observed so that the nomenclature current at the time of printing has been used.

Ten years ago I did hope that *Ferns* would entertain as well as inform the reader. With this new edition, I still hold onto that hope because, as in the first edition, there is much else besides horticultural information contained in these pages — some of it is fanciful and just a little fun, but all of it is interesting.

This new edition has many new and attractive photographs and drawings which, I hope, will encourage growers who are familiar with only a few fern varieties to cultivate more, and inform the yet-to-be-converted gardener — and the browser in bookshops and libraries — of the intriguing and beautiful world that is to be found amidst the graceful fronds of a fern.

I have enjoyed writing the new edition of this book about my favourite plants. I wish you enjoyment of it too; and successful gardening.

Gillean Dunk
Bendigo, Victoria
October 1993

CHAPTER 1

INTRODUCTION

Today, a walk through a fern forest is not only a visually delightful experience; it is also a long step back in history to a time when the earth was shrouded in mist, and much of what is now dry land was covered by the seas. In those days, rain was almost constant and temperatures were much milder than they are today; in such a warm, moist atmosphere the early forms of plant life thrived and grew luxuriantly. This was the Carboniferous period, 350 000 000 years ago, when there were no birds and no mammals, and only dinosaurs roamed the earth amidst vegetation that was dominated by the club mosses, quillworts and horsetails. These were giant plants, growing as tall as ten-storey buildings and spreading their fronds high and wide to seek the sunlight beyond the mist. Ferns — giants also when compared to today's plants — grew below, spreading their fronds to capture the light penetrating the canopy.

These plants can still be seen, but on a vastly different scale. Today, ferns dominate, while the club mosses, quillworts and horsetails grow low down in the shade on the forest floor as tiny replicas of their ancestors. This came about towards the end of the Carboniferous period, when the climate altered and drier conditions prevailed. These conditions were uncongenial for plants that depended on abundant water for their regeneration, as did the early forms of plant life. The mist cleared in the drier atmosphere, bringing about changes in the vegetation: plants did not have to grow as large to capture light, and smaller, more highly developed plant families, such as the conifers, pines and their relations, evolved. The giant horsetails, club mosses and quillworts, and most of the giant ferns, did not survive the change. They fell and became the coal seams of today, and only the smaller species continued to flourish on stream edges and moisture-laden mountain sides in the tropical and temperate parts of the world — the lovely places we call 'fern forests'.

This process took hundreds of millions of years, which brings us to the Mesozoic era. This era began about 225 000 000 years ago, by which time modern ferns, with their characteristic fiddleheads and acropetal growth (i.e. the maturing of the leaf tissues from the base towards the tip), were well established. Fossil records of this time show the existence of several families including Marattiaceae, Osmundaceae, Gleicheniaceae and Schizaeaceae, some individual species of which still flourish. Ferns may actually have existed before the Carboniferous period, since fossils from the earlier Devonian period — some 395 000 000 years ago — show vegetation with fern-like characteristics. These remains may have been the ancestors of the 'seed' ferns (which may have been the first seed-bearing plants) as well as our modern fern species. A few of what are known as 'primitive' ferns, like the species of *Angiopteris* and *Psilophyton*, are still with us today.

During their evolutionary process, true ferns have become smaller and more complex. However, their method of reproduction has not changed and, like their allies, they have remained dependent on water for regeneration and have thereby retained a link with their ancestors, the first of the vascular plants, the seaweeds and mosses.

Because of the fern's ability to disperse its dust-like spores, the genus is found in most countries, and species of the same genus — species which may vary slightly or greatly — may be found in several different and widely separated land masses. The distribution of individual fern genera is much greater than that of flowering plants, and may be traced to the prevailing wind and water-flow patterns of the world. Species of the *Nephrolepsis* genus, for example, can be found on every continent. Within individual continents, dispersal patterns may similarly be related to prevailing wind and water patterns — e.g. *Asplenium sepentrionale* on the North American continent.

Ferns have adapted to a surprising variety of habitats. In tropical rainforests, they are most diverse and luxuriant, sometimes dominating the vegetation. In the temperate regions fewer, and different, species are found. The appearance of these species is not as soft nor as luxuriant as that of the tropical rainforest ferns, and on the whole, they are smaller and not as conspicuous. In cool temperate zones, the ferns' fronds are a darker green and of a coarser texture. In the coolest latitudes, and in the highest altitudes of the temperate zones where ferns grow, a drier atmosphere usually prevails and fern species are fewer again; they are sometimes deciduous and invariably smaller and hardier.

Within each of the climatic zones, the individual fern species have adapted to their specific environments. They are found in the arid scrub and in the grasslands of the tropics, where they have adapted to seasonal drought. They grow on exposed coastal cliffs where they are able to tolerate salt spray, and in dry and rocky outcrops where shade, water and humus-rich soil (which are perceived by most to be the normal requirements for ferns to grow) are scant. Several species that are native to high altitudes in temperate zones are able to survive even when they are covered by snow for months of each year. Some species are so hardy that they are able to thrive in the cracks and crevices of city buildings where they tolerate highly polluted air and direct sunlight.

A group of tree ferns — they have a long history dating back 325 million years.

Fossil of *Sphenopteris flexuosa*, 250 million years old, found in Permian rocks.

In such varying environments, ferns have adapted themselves for survival. Some terrestrial species, like those of the *Lygodium* genus, climb towards sunlight; others, like the tree ferns *Cyathea* and *Dicksonia*, have developed tall trunks and large spreading fronds to catch the sunlight. Epiphytes, like the *Platycerium* genus, have developed nest-like leaves to trap falling vegetation, which eventually rots and turns into humus.

A few ferns, like some of the *Doryopteris* and *Cheilanthes* species, are xerophytes. They have developed unique mechanisms to withstand long periods of drought. Their small tough fronds are covered with minute hairs, which give them a silvery or woolly appearance and protect them from strong sunlight and loss of moisture.

Aquatic ferns, such as *Azolla*, and those that are semi-aquatic, such as *Marsilea*, have evolved small scale-like or clover-shaped fronds which enable them to float on the water's surface. In this environment, the *Marsilea* has also made an evolutionary 'leap' by developing a more advanced reproductive mechanism than any other fern (see p. 167).

The filmy ferns — e.g. the *Hymenophyllum* and *Trichomanes* genera — have hardly any structure to their fronds, so that the delicate tissues, which are no wider than a single cell, are able to absorb water directly from the moisture-laden air of their natural habitat. Other fern species have also developed interesting survival mechanisms: e.g. *Polypodium bifrons* has water-storing sacs for times of drought, and the well-known *Nephrolepis cordifolia* var. *tuberosa* carries food-storing tubers on modified aerial roots.

CLASSIFICATION

The plant kingdom is divided into two main groups — *phanerogams*, the seed-bearing plants, and *cryptogams*, the non-seed-bearing plants. (Ferns are cryptogams.) These two great subkingdoms are divided into classes, orders, families, genera and species. It is interesting to look at some of these divisions, because through them we may be able to see the evolution of plant life, and sometimes, the reasons for a particular plant's demise or for its survival.

Cryptogams are divided into three groups:

- The *thallophytes*, a group of about 125 000 species of the most primitive plants found on earth — the algae and the fungi.
- The *bryophytes*, a group of about 20 000 species of mosses and liverworts. These are more highly developed than the thallophytes in that they have a hair-like appendage known as a rhizoid, which anchors the plant to the ground and absorbs water with a capillary-like action. The rhizoid, however, is not a true root as it cannot absorb nutrients.
- The *pteridophytes*, a group of about 10 000 species to which true ferns and their allies belong. While there are many different forms of ferns within this group, all reproduce by means of spores and all are true vascular plants. (Vascular plants contain bundles of vein tissue which conduct water and nutrients to all parts of the plant.) Thus, this group represents a major evolutionary advance.

The floor of a fern forest, Victoria, Australia.

The four divisions of the pteridophytes reflect further evolutionary advances from the primitive plant forms of the Psilotinae division (fork ferns), through the Lycopodinae division (club mosses, selanginellas and quillworts) and Sphenopsida class (horsetails), to the most highly developed, the Filicineae class — the class to which all true ferns belong. Further divisions into orders, families, genera and species thereafter, reflect the smaller, more subtle changes that ferns have made in adapting themselves to their environment.

The major characteristics by which ferns (and indeed all plants) are identified are their reproductive process and the structure of their reproductive parts. (A casual observer should not be misled into thinking that plants — whether seed-bearing plants or ferns — that have similar leaves, fronds, flowers etc., necessarily belong to the same species.) In most seed-bearing plants both the reproductive process and structure are conspicuous; in all ferns, both are so minute as to only be visible under magnification.

THE STRUCTURE OF FERNS

Though it is not the purpose of this book to provide a strict botanical description by which ferns can be identified, some introduction to their specialised structure is essential. Ferns are a unique group of plants with a unique set of botanical terms to describe them.

What is called the stem in other plants, i.e. the part that is leaf-bearing on top and root-producing on the bottom, is referred to as the *rhizome*. The rhizome creeps above or under the ground, or clings to a support, or it can grow erect. When it forms a trunk, as it does in tree ferns, the trunk is called a *caudex*.

The leaves, which in ferns are called *fronds*, emerge from the rhizome or the caudex. They may be either undivided (simple), divided (compound) or highly divided (decompound). (Botanists classify fronds as leaf-like expansions in which the functions of the stem and foliage are not completely differentiated.) It is characteristic of all ferns, except the Ophiglossalceae family, that the embryonic fronds are curled and unroll as they grow, and that they are covered by scales or hair. There are two types

Angiopteris evecta, a 'living fern fossil'. Fossil remains that are 300 million years old may be its ancestors.

of fronds: either spore-bearing and fertile, or infertile. The two may look alike or they may emphasise their different functions with different shapes (dimorphic) and postures; however, to aid in the dispersal of the spores, the fertile frond usually stands more erect than the infertile.

The lower part of the stalk, from the rhizome to the base of the leaf blade or *lamina*, is called a *stipe*. Beyond this, where it forms the midrib of fronds, it is called a *rachis*. A branch from the rachis, as occurs in divided fronds, is called a *secondary rachis*. If there is a further branching from the secondary rachis, this is called a *tertiary rachis.*

Regarding the lamina, there are two types of laminar structure. One is composed of *lobes* where the divisions of the lamina do not extend to the rachis. The other is composed of *pinnae*, the small leaflets formed when the divisions of the lamina do reach the rachis. If a pinna is divided into yet smaller segments, these are called *pinnules*.

Spores form in a case known as a *sporangium*, and where these cluster together they are called *sori*. It is the sori that are generally visible to the naked eye. They are first seen as light green indentations on the back of the fronds. As they ripen over a few months, they form raised clusters in colours varying from light rusty brown through the deep rich browns to almost black. The sori usually form patterns; when these are obvious, they are a means by which a casual observer can distinguish a fern from other plants. The patterns may take the form of either random or precise dots, or lines; they may form bands of felt-like ribbons around the perimeter or along the main veins of the pinna; or they may cover the entire undersurface. In some species, the patterns are not obvious.

The sori may be covered by a thin membrane called an *indusium*, or the margin of the leaf itself may be rolled over to protect those sori that form on the edge — this is known as a *false indusium*. As the sori mature, the indusium shrinks, and it is eventually shed when the spore cases are ready to open and release the spores.

The sporangia can be seen easily with a hand lens. They are rounded or egg-shaped capsules on delicate stalks. Each capsule is banded or, in some cases, marked by a ring of cells of a much tougher consistency than the cells that make up the spore cases. This ring of cells, called

Osmunda regalis, growing in its favourite habitat, over water.

Divided or compound frond.

an *annulus*, contracts and tears at a certain stage of dehydration, thereby opening the case and ejecting the spores. The 'lid' immediately snaps back into place, almost closing the case. There may be several dozen sporangia in each cluster of sori, and each sporangia produces an even number of spores — usually 64. The number of spores produced by a fern in its lifetime may be in the millions.

The spores are like dust, so it is impossible to see their structure without a high-powered magnifying glass. Such magnification shows that they are bean-shaped or pyramid-shaped according to species, and that they vary in colour from green to black, and in texture from smooth to wrinkled. Some are spotted, some are plain. All are made up of a single cell. The fern that each spore will eventually produce may grow to be the size of a tuft of grass or a majestic palm, but initially, each spore is almost indistinguishable from another and is always microscopic in size.

LIFE CYCLE

The reproductive cycle of the fern was not understood by botanists until the middle of the 19th century. It was assumed that, like all known plants, it went through the usual processes of fertilisation and the development of a seed. However, because the seed — if it did exist — was 'invisible', this seemingly 'magical' ability to regenerate was surrounded by superstition and credited with supernatural properties.

The fern's life cycle is not magical, but it is one of the most interesting in the plant world. It is vastly different to that of a flower-bearing plant.

The reproductive process of flowering plants is clearly visible in the highly complex forms of their flowers, fruit and seeds, and in the adaptation of their seeds to distribution that is dependent on wind, water, insects, birds and animals. In contrast, the fern's reproductive process is much simpler. The fern is totally dependent on water for regeneration and shows a continuous link with the earliest beginnings of life on Earth, which began in water.

The fern requires two alternating generations to complete its life cycle: a sexual *(gametophyte)* generation and a non-sexual *(sporophyte)* generation.

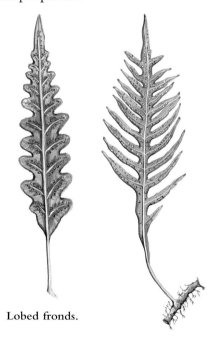

Lobed fronds.

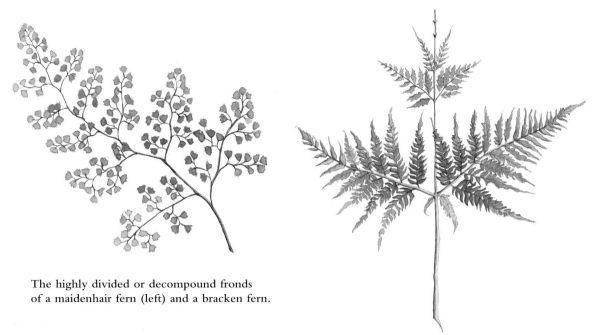

The highly divided or decompound fronds
of a maidenhair fern (left) and a bracken fern.

The frond-bearing plant that we instantly recognise and call a 'fern' is the sporophyte. It is this plant's function to produce a minute spore which, when ripe and in a suitable environment, will develop into a tiny plant called a *prothallus*.

Let us first consider the spore. It is actually the germ of a new plant — one very different from its parent. It has little in common with the seed of a flowering plant, differing both in its structure and its pattern of growth. The spore is a single cell that commences growth with its enlargement and multiplication. It must form its own structures that are capable of seeking water and nutrients in the soil, and of seeking light, in order to manufacture food by photosynthesis. Whichever part of the growing organism touches the soil will form roots; whichever part lies uppermost will form a shoot.

By contrast, a seed is a rudimentary plant that will grow to be a replica of its parent. It consists of two organisms: a *radicle*, the germ of a future root, and a *plumule*, the germ of a future shoot. Wherever, or however, a seed falls, there is no change in the respective functions of these two parts: the radicle will go down into the soil and the plumule will grow up to the source of light and air. It has its own reserves of food on which to draw until roots and shoots begin to function.

Unlike a germinating seed, the prothallus that develops from the spore is a delicate organism. It has no reserves and, like a mature plant, in adverse conditions it may die. Like a seed, however, both

Undivided or
simple frond.

the spore and the prothallus may live on for years until conditions for growth — and in the case of the prothallus, for the fertilisation of the eggs that it contains — are suitable.

The prothallus is the fern's sexual stage of growth and contains the reproductive organs. If sufficient moisture is present, fertilisation takes place and the second generation plant, the sporophyte, grows. In time this 'new' plant will mature and bear spores.

Once a spore begins to grow, it requires the same conditions as the mature fern. If any one of the millions of spores released by the sporophyte comes to rest on a shaded moist place when these conditions are present, it will begin to grow. The tough outer wall of the single spore cell bursts and divides in two. One part becomes a root, or *rhizoid*, which as the cells continue to divide, grows downwards to anchor the plant and seek water. The second part of the original cell grows lengthways into a long green thread of single cells. After about one week, this ribbon of cells has sent down its own rhizoids to maintain itself; the wedge-shaped cells at the growing tip have sent out lateral growth; and the prothallus, as it is now called, has taken on its characteristic heart shape. Prior to this stage, the growing prothalli appear only as fine green scum on the surface of the soil.

After about 12 weeks growth, individual plants are visible to the naked eye. Each plant appears as a delicate, almost translucent, membrane with the horizontal dimension of a small coin and the vertical dimension of only a few cells. Fine root hairs can be seen on its undersurface, and with the aid of a microscope, the many male and female parts, which also develop on the underside and are called the *antheridia* and the *archegonia* respectively, can be seen.

Each archegonium consists of a group of cells in the shape of a flask and contains a single egg. When this is ripe, the flask bursts open and secretes a malic acid which activates and attracts the *antherozoids* (sperm) that have now formed in great numbers in the antheridia. The antheridia mature before the archegonia, increasing the chance that one of the prothalli will be fertilised by sperm from another prothallus. A high potential for genetic variation within the species, and for cross-fertilisation from other species, is thus maintained.

The bursting open of the archegonia is a surprising, animal-like action. What is even more surprising — considering this is the plant world — is that the sperm are

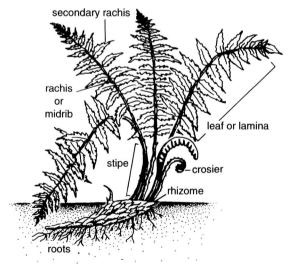

A fern sporophyte — the second generation plant that will produce spores.

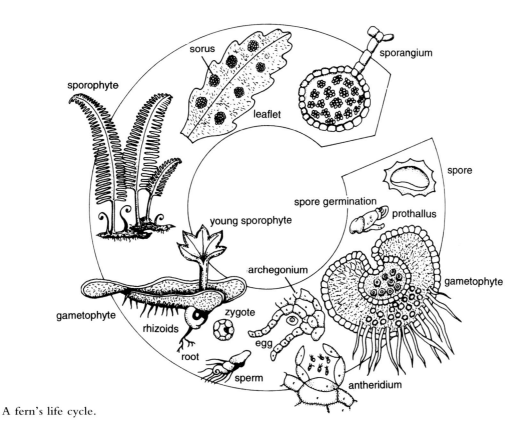

A fern's life cycle.

motile and actually swim to the egg. Moisture is essential: the antheridia can open and release sperm only when in contact with water and sperm can move only in water. The sperm are minute thread-like organisms with a bladder-like head and a coiled tail; the tail is covered with tiny hairs which rotate and propel the sperm along in a spinning motion. This form of fertilisation by motile sperm takes place in all lower plants — the ferns, mosses, horsetails and quillworts.

The sperm are attracted to, and swim down the neck of, the archegonium. Again animal-like, only one sperm penetrates and fertilises the egg. At this point the growth of the fern, as we recognise it, begins — a 'grandchild' as it were. The new plant (the sporophyte) is contained within and protected by the archegonium, and draws on the prothallus for food until it develops rhizoids of its own and the prothallus is withered and gone, its work done.

The first signs of growth of the sporophyte that are visible to the naked eye are the embryonic fronds, which are usually simple in shape and quite unlike the fronds that are characteristic of the mature fern; in all but a few species, they unfurl from the characteristic crosier-like buds. The new fern gradually assumes the form and habit of the 'grandparent' and, when mature, produces fronds which carry spores. Then the whole fascinating life cycle starts again.

CHAPTER 2

A HISTORY OF FERNS

A mythology has been built up around ferns in certain societies; and, in many parts of the world, they have been and still are used by humans as a source of food and building materials. However, it was the English, during the Victorian era, who were the first keen collectors of ferns, and who first appreciated the graceful foliage as decorative features in their homes. In a way, ferns were the first indoor plants of modern society.

Fern collecting dates back several centuries to 1628, when John Tradescant, who owned a botanical garden and museum at Lambeth in London, brought some new plants back from a voyage he had taken to Virginia, in America. Among them were two ferns — *Cystopteris bulbifera* (berry or bulblet bladder fern) and *Adiantum pedatum* (American maidenhair). In 1680, he added another fern from America, *Camptosorus rhizophyllum* (walking fern); and some years later, yet another, *Onoclea sensibilis* (bead fern), as well as two from Madeira, *Adiantum reniforme* and *Davallia canariensis* (Canary Island hare's foot fern). The only other recorded fern in England at that time was *Blechnum australe*; this fern had already been noted in King Charles II's garden at Hampton Court in 1671.

At the beginning of the 18th century there were no more than five species of exotic ferns in Britain. But by the 1770s fern collecting had gained popularity with botanists, and between 1770 and 1790, 68 species were being cultivated in private collections and in the official collection of the Royal Botanic Gardens at Kew.

The now world famous Royal Botanic Gardens at Kew, in the London Borough of Richmond, were first planted in 1759 as a hobby of King George III's mother. Later that century, they came under the patronage of Sir Joseph Banks, the wealthy gentleman-botanist who accompanied Captain James Cook on his first voyage to the Pacific in 1768–71. Banks was greatly stimulated by these travels, and on his return to England, made great efforts to organise the collecting of new and rare plants for the Gardens by persuading the commanders of warships and the traders who travelled to the East Indies to take an interest in botany. As a result of their

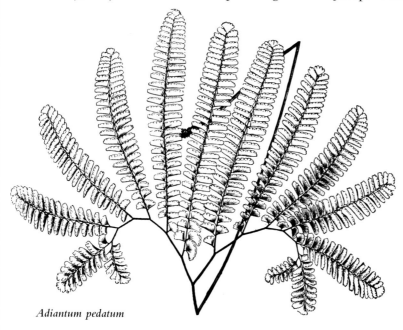

Adiantum pedatum

efforts, many new plants were added to the Kew collection — some in the form of dried specimens; some as seeds; and the few that survived the long sea voyages, as living specimens. *Hortus Kewensis*, a list of plants and general botanical guide that was first published by the Gardens in 1768, listed ten ferns among its new exotic plants; the second edition, published in 1789, listed 34 ferns. In 1793, following the return of HMS *Providence*, then under the command of Rear-Admiral William Bligh, from its second voyage to the British colonies in the West Indies, 37 new plants were added to the fern collection. (William Bligh contributed greatly to the scientific knowledge of

Trichomanes radicans

his time, which, regrettably, has been largely overlooked because of two unfortunate incidents in his career: the mutiny on his ship, HMS *Bounty*, in 1789; and some years later, the Rum Rebellion in the then penal colony of New South Wales, Australia, while he was Governor.)

In 1808, the first ferns from Australia were taken to England by George Caley. Caley, a one-time horse doctor from Birmingham, had been commissioned by Sir Joseph Banks to collect plants in New South Wales for the Royal Botanical Gardens. Among the ferns he sent back were *Platycerium bifurcatum* (staghorn or elkhorn fern), *Doodia aspera* (prickly rasp fern) and *Davallia pyxidata* (a species of hare's, rabbit's or squirrel's foot fern). In 1816, another official collector, Alan Cunningham, sent several more species from Australia, and the first species from Norfolk Island, then a British penal colony off the east coast of Australia. He was a veteran collector, having already spent several years in Brazil with James Rowie, another collector for the Gardens.

JOHN SMITH
AND THE KEW COLLECTION

By the middle of the 1800s, exotic plants were arriving constantly at the Royal Botanical Gardens at Kew from the British colonies and other places. Their arrival was always well publicised and attracted crowds of interested spectators. By this time, the Gardens had an impressive collection of ferns under the devoted care of John Smith, curator of the Gardens for 40 years. Smith was a fern enthusiast, and was responsible for acquiring most of the ferns in the Gardens.

From its beginnings under the patronage of Sir Joseph Banks, the fern collection had been eclectic but not large; it had certainly not been in good hands. In the early 1800s, half the specimens it contained were from the West Indies; four came from the Cape of Good Hope; three from Australia, then called New Holland; and one from St Helena — the British island in the Atlantic that was the scene of Napoleon's last exile. The rest were from North America and Madeira. When John Smith took over as curator in 1822, he lamented that only 40 of the original exotic ferns remained in the collection and that the surviving species were in poor condition, with the tropical species being almost non-existent.

This had occurred because the flues on the brick fireplaces used for heating the Gardens' hothouses had been badly constructed, so that they leaked smoke and dried out the atmosphere, making it unsuitable for the good cultivation, or even preservation, of the fern collection. Smith renovated the hothouses, and organised the Gardens' entire collection of plants so well that Kew became the most important botanical centre in Great Britain. By 1846, he was able to announce proudly that there were 348 species in the fern houses.

Among those ferns which attracted particular interest because of their novelty were some of the first species to arrive from Australia. *Grammitis billardieri* (finger fern), sent to Kew in 1833 by the Sydney Botanic Gardens, and *Platycerium superbum* (staghorn, elkhorn or moosehorn fern), sent by the botanic gardens in Brisbane a little later, were regarded as great curiosities — the finger fern because of its entire fronds and the *Platycerium* species because of its epiphytal growth.

The first tree ferns to arrive at the Royal Botanical Gardens in Kew were sent by a New

Tea cup with fern motif.

Zealand gardener, J. Edgerly, in 1841, and caused great excitement when they arrived. The two ferns, *Dicksonia squarrosa* (rough dicksonia or wheki fern) and *Cyathea medullaris* (korau, mamaku or black tree fern) were immediately in great demand. In 1866, they were described in the British press as the feature of an international exhibition in the Crystal Palace, 'rearing their magnificent heads above the gorgeous collection of azaleas, roses etc. — indeed, but for the tree ferns, the exhibition would have lacked half its beauty and attraction as no other plants we have in cultivation would have substituted'. These particular 'majestic specimens' were later destroyed in a fire in the tropical section of the Crystal Palace.

John Smith not only contributed to the collection and cultivation of ferns, he also did a great deal to promote their popularity by publishing two books and regularly listing the new acquisitions of the Gardens. He publicised Kew as the botanical centre of Europe, and being somewhat jealous of his reputation as a collector, personally inspected

A Victorian interior — ferns decorated the drawing rooms of all social classes.

a large collection in Berlin to compare it with his own. He was not impressed. On his return to England, he suggested, not indiscreetly, that the size of the Berlin collection had been exaggerated. He was kinder to his British colleagues, however, and acted as their patron. He conscientiously listed ferns in both private and public gardens and maintained a friendly rivalry with other collectors and writers, as they did with him — it was, after all, a gentlemanly pursuit.

THE VICTORIAN ERA

By 1857, John Smith's *Catalogue of Cultivated Ferns* listed 560 species in British gardens. The Victorian era had begun and plant collecting, which had come under the patronage of the Crown and wealthy, scientifically minded gentlemen, was considered a suitable hobby for any genteel person. Ferns were the most popular plants with collectors. They were also much sought after as decorations for the drawing rooms of the wealthy and humble alike, their bright luxuriant foliage appealing to the then fashionable taste for elaborate decoration.

> *No fête, horticultural exhibition, banquet or public dinner was successful*
> *without ferns to grace the occasion, for gay and brilliant colours alone will not*
> *satisfy the eyes of the horticultural public. Some happy change has come about*
> *in respect to floral exhibitions, also in the decoration of our gardens at home,*
> *both indoors and out — the rule being that flowering plants must have mixed*
> *with them a certain amount of ornamental foliage or the effect is not pleasing to*
> *the eye. Some, indeed, assert that a conservatory properly arranged with*
> *ornamental foliage plants and ferns alone, is the most effective.*

So wrote B. S. Williams, a well-known fern grower, collector and writer, in his *Select Ferns and Cycopods* published in 1873.

Wealthy collectors built conservatories made of leaded glass to house their collections. Sometimes these were attached to the house as an elegant extension of the parlour. Alternatively, a small ornamental case was permanently fixed to a windowsill. Those who could not afford a conservatory kept their precious collections in Wardian cases (decorative glass-panelled cases of varying sizes and styles) or under the glass shades that were also popular for covering the wax fruit, stuffed birds and other curiosities so dear to the Victorians.

The wider use of glass in the cultivation of plants had been made possible in 1845, when the duty on sheet glass was lifted, making it a cheap commodity. By 1851, the spectacular Crystal Palace, built in London to house the Exhibition of 1851, had brought the material to popular attention, and also the potential for it to be used in the cultivation and attractive display of plants. With the ready availability of glass at moderate prices and the copious supply of a large variety of ferns from nurseries and street hawkers, fern cultivation was brought within the reach of many. In Britain, even the 'hard-working mechanic' had a fernery, a fact alluded to by John Smith in his book *Ferns: British and Foreign* (1866).

In the United States of America in 1860, hanging baskets of ferns were reported as being popular amongst the fashionable. However, when these later became as 'common in the tenement of the mechanic as in the palaces on Fifth Avenue' (*Decorative Art of Victoria's Era* by Frances Litchen, 1950), it was noted that the determinedly fashionable were keeping their collections under glass, so maintaining their exclusiveness.

Fern collecting and cultivation stayed in vogue for over half a century in Britain, Europe and North America. No other plant — not even the tulip, which had been popular for many years during the 18th century — remained fashionable for quite so long. The heaths, proteas, aloes and other 'curiosities' from the New World, in particular Australia and South Africa, were eagerly taken up by botanists, but were discarded just as quickly. The more showy and easily cultivated varieties of cacti from the New World

A Victorian conservatory, with ferns growing amongst palms, yuccas and cordylines.

remained in vogue with keen collectors for longer, although John Smith, in one of his books about ferns, dismissed them as 'scarcely saleable'. He also dismissed orchids as too difficult and too expensive to cultivate, and as being 'confined for the most part to the gardens of the wealthy'. Ferns, he suggested, could be grown, as a general rule, in a comparatively inexpensive manner. But then he was a fern enthusiast!

Sadly, the Victorian fern craze has left behind an unwelcome legacy. At the height of the craze, commercial growers and amateur collectors scoured the English countryside for the indigenous species. So thorough was their collecting that many believe the English countryside has never quite recovered from this vandalism. *Adiantum capillus-veneris* (green petticoat fern) and *Adiantum ceterach* (rusty back or scaly spleenwort) are now found in fewer numbers in their natural habitat because of this overzealous collecting.

The popularity of ferns as house plants began to decline with the introduction of gas heating and lighting. Even though the Victorians understood the ferns' levels of tolerance for indoor conditions, and carefully removed their plants to ferneries and glasshouses to revive them, the poisonous fumes and the dry atmosphere created by the new heating appliances were too severe, and ferns were gradually replaced by hardier varieties of plants, such as aspidistras and yuccas. Out of doors, though, in graceful little conservatories, contrived grottoes and miniature rockery landscapes, they were still widely cultivated and much admired.

The turn of the century and the Edwardian era brought more changes: tastes in decoration had become much simpler and ferns, so evocative of the Victorians' taste for elaborate ornamentation, were no longer acceptable in the home. Still greater changes were not far away. The austerities of the Great War period of 1914–18 resulted in many British public and private gardens being ploughed and sown with vegetables to feed the people and the soldiers of the beleaguered country. This ended the widespread growing of beautiful and exotic plants for pleasure until much later in the century. Few nurseries and private gardens were to grow ferns again on the same scale practised during the Victorian era.

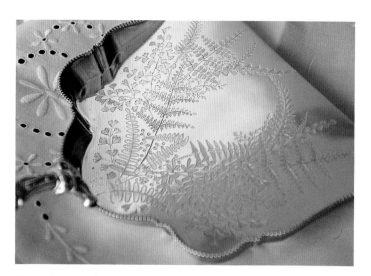

Victorian crumb tray with fern motif.

The Great Conservatory Showhouse, London, England.

Wardian Cases and Fern Shades

Wardian cases and glass shades were popular in Victorian times with collectors and with those who used the fashionable plants as ornaments in their homes. The cases and shades re-created the conditions inside a glasshouse, providing an ideal atmosphere for plants that required protection and humidity. Growers were able to utilise these 'miniature greenhouses' to maintain and increase their collections, many of which by this time comprised exotic species from the tropical and warm temperate parts of the world.

A glass shade or 'closed case'.

Nathaniel Bagshaw Ward, an eminent surgeon in London in the 1830s, has been credited with the invention of the Wardian case, although this has been challenged. In the 18th century, a botanist, William Withering, had already devised something resembling the Wardian case for the transportation of living plant specimens. This was a small jar, which contained water, set inside a larger, sealed jar. Another botanist, A. A. Maconochie, a Scot and a contemporary of Ward's, also

A typical Wardian case, made by Eade and Son.

anticipated Ward's 'discovery' when he found that he could successfully grow ferns and club mosses in a large glass container that had previously been used for goldfish. Being a true gentleman, Maconochie graciously never claimed his lead in this important scientific discovery, but rather, conceded its accreditation and naming to Ward.

Ward was himself a true Victorian gentleman who studied all the sciences, but botany was his hobby and ferns his favourite plant. He had tried in vain to grow ferns and mosses on an old wall at his home in Finsbury Circus, which was a particularly smoggy part of London, described by Ward as 'surrounded by numerous manufactories and enveloped in their smoke'. He was about to give up his ambitions in the face of such adverse conditions when he was 'led to reflect a little more deeply upon the subject in consequence of a simple incident which occurred in the summer of 1829'. He recounted:

> I had buried the chrysalis of a sphinx (moth) in some moist mould contained in a wide-mouthed glass bottle, covered with a lid. In watching the bottle from day to day, I observed that the moisture that during the heat of the day arose from the mould, became condensed on the internal surface of the glass, and returned whence it came, thus keeping the mould always in the same degree of humidity. Almost a week prior to the final changes of the insect, a seedling fern and a grass made their appearance on the surface of the mould. I could not but be struck with the circumstance of one of that very tribe of plants, which I had for years fruitlessly attempted to cultivate, coming up sponte sua in such a situation; and asked myself seriously what were the conditions necessary for its growth. To this the answer was — firstly, an atmosphere free from soot; secondly, light; thirdly, heat; fourthly, moisture and lastly, air.

Ward's simple bottle evolved into the functional, ornamental and fashionable Wardian case, in which keen fern growers were able to cultivate a wide range of species, especially those requiring warmth and high humidity. Such was the importance of Ward's discovery to the fern growers of the time that the original bottle, with the still unwatered plants inside, was put on display at the Great Exhibition in London in 1851, and Ward was elected a Fellow of the Royal Society. Wardian cases were widely used by botanists on exploratory expeditions to send new and live plants back to the fascinated British public, who flocked to see the new arrivals at the Royal Botanic Gardens at Kew.

> *It is a bit of the woodside sealed down with the life of the wood in it, and when unsealed for a moment it gives forth an odour that might delude us into the belief that we have been suddenly wafted to some dusky dell where the nodding violet grows.*

This charming quote comes from a keen Victorian botanist, Shirley Hibberd, in his book, *The Rambling Botanist*. He was an enthusiastic fern grower and wrote many books on the subject. In one of them, he modestly but proudly claims that his wife's fernery had 'nothing in England to surpass it in beauty and interest — though it is on an extremely small scale'.

Hibberd experimented a great deal with growing ferns in sealed glass cases and had some very definite ideas on the art, which he set forth categorically in his many books. Although successful in growing ferns, he did experience some setbacks. He advised growers to ensure that the glass dome fitted loosely into the pan that accompanied it after one such experience. One of his shades, 'which was a tight fit, was one day removed to a sunny window for some domestic operations. The sun heated the air within the shade, the expanded air had no means to escape, and it burst the shade with a loud explosion into a multitude of fragments. A guinea's worth of glass was thus lost in a moment and a collection of selaginellas placed in jeopardy through neglect of this precaution.'

Mr Rosher's patented fern pillar.

Hibberd's glass dome was only one of the many types of fern shades and Wardian cases available at the time. With glass a relatively cheap commodity, inventors found numerous ways to use it for scientific purposes. This included creating a range of fern shades.

The simplest form of fern shade was a glass dome that sat snugly on a modified flower pot.

It was invented by a Mr Fry and made by a potter, Mr Pascall, of Chiselhurst, England. The pot was of fine terracotta — sometimes roughly ornamented — and had a wide shallow rim. The glass shade, with a knob on top, was fitted into the rim and water poured around it, thus making it airtight. These fern shades were rather small, no more than 40 cm (15 in) high, and were considered a very attractive table decoration.

A further refinement of this principle was a glass shade that rested on a matching glass dish — a Mr Rosher's patented idea. Larger versions of this shade sometimes contained an ornamented pillar of fine porcelain with holes around the sides. The holes were filled with damp compost and planted with tiny ferns and mosses, which were trimmed regularly so that the pillar was always visible. Even more elegant were the versions that contained a pillar topped with a miniature Grecian urn filled with a small cascading fern. Such arrangements must have looked very attractive under their fragile glass domes, but the upkeep would have been constant.

Larger collections of ferns were housed in Wardian cases, which contained a watertight metal trough to hold soil; some had leg supports so that they were independent pieces of furniture; some had castors so that they could be moved easily to

A teapot with fern motif.

Wrought-iron lace in a fern design.

take advantage of the daylight. In true Victorian style, they became more and more elaborate over time, both in their design and their ornamentation, until some fern growers had virtual miniature Crystal Palaces standing in their parlours.

Cases known as 'Miss Maling's' were the most popular. They had simple rectangular outlines and could be heated with hot water, renewed periodically. Patented cases made by Gray of Danvers Street, Chelsea, in London, had the optional extra of a boiler to provide the plants with warmth. The manufacturer claimed that the boiler was 'efficient' and needed to be filled only once or twice a day during winter — fern growers obviously needed to be very dedicated.

Inside the cases, the artistic grower created fern landscapes in miniature. The recommended material for rocks was coke, which added little weight. The secret of making coke look like rock was to soak it in water and sprinkle it with a little Roman or Portland cement. Lichen and moss soon grew on the surface to enhance the naturalness of the overall effect.

But Shirley Hibberd was to sound a note of warning regarding 'the niceties of gimcrackery — the grand thing is to have a sufficiency of healthy ferns of handsome varieties, everything else must be made subsidiary to that desideratum'.

USES OF FERNS

The fronds of ferns are made up of mucilaginous and slightly astringent tissues, the fleshier parts of which contain starch. The rhizomes also contain starch and are bitter, acrid and astringent. Over the centuries, these properties have been exploited by humans, mainly as a source of food and medicine.

The economic usefulness of ferns has never been significant. In one of the few commercial ventures that did make use of ferns, the first European settlers in Fiji and

Hawaii (then called the Sandwich Islands) used the fibres covering the stipes of some ferns, which were native to these islands, to fill their pillows, finding the vegetable matter stayed cooler than feathers in the sultry tropical climate. Enterprising settlers in the Sandwich Islands exported the silky fibres of the native species of the *Cibotium* genus as a filling material. The business venture was short-lived. The fibres collapsed with use, and the trade, consequently, with them.

As Food

As a source of food, ferns have been used in the past mainly by the indigenous people of particular countries, some of whom still use them today. In New Zealand, the Maoris baked the soft pith of the tree fern *Cyathea medullaris* (korau, mamaku or black tree fern) to a reddish brown before consuming it. They also used the large swollen scaly rhizomes of the *Marattia salicina* (potato fern) and the rhizomes of another of their native ferns, *Pteridium esculentum* (Australian or common bracken), which they roasted in ashes, peeled with their teeth and ate, rather like a bread. (Readers are advised not to eat this fern as it is now known to contains carcinogens.) The Aborigines of New South Wales, in Australia, ate the *Blechnum cartilagineum* (bristle fern) rhizome, said to taste rather like a waxy potato; it was roasted then beaten to break down the woody fibre.

Pteridium aquilinum, a bracken once eaten in Europe.

In New Caledonia, the indigenous people extracted the soft pith at the base of the fronds of the tree fern, *Cyathea vieillardii*, for food. In the nearby Society Islands, the young shoots of the king fern, *Angiopteris evecta*, were eaten by the indigenous people, who also made flour from its large rhizome. The young fronds of the *Helminthostachys zeylanica* (flowering fern) were also prepared and eaten in the same way as asparagus.

The islanders of the Indian Archipelago still eat the succulent fronds of their curious native water fern, *Ceratopteris thalictroides*. Similarly, when food is scarce in the Fijian islands, the Fijians eat the young fronds of their native fern *Alsophila lunulata* (balabala).

Today, a taste for ferns as food is considered exotic in some countries, and commonplace in others. Australians and New Zealanders would be surprised to find ferns for sale in their food markets, whereas in North America and Southeast Asia, they are quite commonplace. Americans and Canadians are able to buy the fiddleheads of their native fern, *Matteuccia struthioptris* (ostrich fern), either fresh, frozen or canned. The Four Seasons Restaurant in New York regularly offers 'fiddleheads *au gratin*' as a seasonal delicacy on its spring menu. (The recipe for this dish is published in the *Four Seasons Cookbook* (1971) by Charlotte Adams, who describes the fiddleheads as 'unique in flavour and delightful in appearance'. They are blanched and mixed with a béchamel sauce, then sprinkled with cheese and browned under a grill or broiler.) Similarly, the edible fern native to Southeast Asia, *Diplazium esculentum*,

Dryopteris filix-mas, popular as a boiled vegetable in Norway.

which grows prolifically on the banks of streams, is found for sale in the food markets of Indonesia and Malaysia. In western Java, where the fern is called 'pakis', the fronds are steamed and served with rice and a chilli sauce, or chopped and made into soup.

From left: *Adiantum capillus-veneris*, which is used to make a tea, and *A. aethiopicum*.

Of the European countries, Norway is the only one that still consistently uses ferns as a type of food. There, the young, tender crosiers of *Dryopteris filix-mas* (male fern) are popular as a boiled vegetable. This particular fern, together with *Pteridium esculentum* (common bracken), was used in the past throughout Europe in the brewing of ale. Apparently it imparted a unique flavour to the ale. Proportions used in the manufacturing process were one part of the bracken's rhizome to two parts of malt. A less potent beverage — tea — is still made in Europe from the fronds of *Dryopteris fragrans*. In California, in the United States, an extract made from *Pellaea ornithopus* is a popular aromatic herbal tea. Another brew popular throughout the world is made from the fronds of *Adiantum capillus-veneris* (southern maidenhair or Venus's hair fern).

For Medicinal Purposes

Over the centuries, the same mucilagenous, starchy and astringent qualities that have made ferns useful as food have also made them effective medicines. Many references are found to ferns in ancient herbals, and many ferns have acquired their common names through their association with herbal medicines of the past. Like many ancient remedies, some of those made from ferns were, and still are, quite effective; on the other hand, some are merely fanciful, especially when their supposed curing properties involve the supernatural. Then there are those that are both effective and fanciful.

Culpeper, on the properties of *Dryopteris filix-mas* (male fern), wrote in *The English Physitian* (1826): 'It is under the dominion of Mercury . . . being burned, the smoke thereof driveth away serpents, gnats and other noisome creatures, which in fenny countries, do in the nightime, trouble and molest people lying in their beds with their faces uncovered.' The Greek botanist Dioscorides recommended *Botrychium lunaria* (moonwort) in the first century AD 'against the stinging and biting of serpents'. In more recent times — the early 20th century — a folk remedy called 'Adder's Spear Ointment' was used for the bites of 'adders and other reptiles'.

From left: *Asplenium fontanum, A. ruta-muraria, A. trichomanes* and *Ceterach officinarum.*

We can deal with the stings and bites of serpents, adders and sundry reptiles in other ways these days. However, there are some fern remedies that do have important remedial qualities. Ferns have always been regarded as an effective vermifuge (a cure for intestinal worms). Both *Dryopteris filix-mas* (male fern) and *Pteridium esculentum* (common bracken) have powerfully astringent medicinal properties and have been used since the days of Dioscorides as a vermifuge. The medicine was made from the dried and powdered root stock, mixed with honey or syrup, and administered as an electuary. (Again, readers are warned not to use the common brackens as they are now known to contain carcinogens.)

Asplenium is another fern genus that takes its common name — spleenwort — from ancient remedies. The species of this genus were considered useful for liver complaints and 'swellings of the spleen', particularly *Asplenium ceterach*, which resembles a spleen in form. *Asplenium trichomanes* (common maidenhair spleenwort) had additional uses. It was once used in the Scottish Highlands in the form of a tea, for curing coughs and colds, and in the 17th century,

Botrychium lunaria

herbalists recommended it to counter the loss of hair. *Asplenium ceterach*, similarly diverse in usage, was used as a bait for rock cod by fishermen on parts of the Welsh coast. If the fishing was not good, they could be consoled by boiling and eating the roots of the same fern as it was considered a remedy for 'all melancholy' — another recommendation of Culpeper's.

Asplenium ruta-muraria (wall rue) once had the curious name 'tentwort', which may have come from its being used in the treatment of rickets — a disease formerly called 'taint'. At the beginning of the 20th century, in parts of the Cumberland County in England, *Osmunda regalis* (royal fern) was also a popular remedy for this disease. The royal fern was thought to possess other healing qualities; it could be applied externally, or taken as a decoction to aid in the healing of wounds, bruises, sprains and broken bones.

Ferns also appear in Asian medicine. In northern Asia, scurvy (caused by a lack of vitamin C) was treated with a medication made from the fronds of *Dryopteris fragrans*. The herbarium of the British Museum has ancient specimens of the rhizomes of a species of *Davallia* used in Chinese medical practice. In India, *Nothalaena piloselloides* was used to reduce sponginess of the gums. In Java, a medicine called 'penghawar-djambi', made from the hairs on the lower stipes of the native species of *Dicksonia* and *Cibotium* ferns, was used as a styptic, to check bleeding. This medicine is listed in a German pharmacopoeia of the 19th century.

FOLKLORE

In times past, the powers to impart invisibility, unshoe horses, unlock doors, fend off the devil and his minions, and change mercury into silver have all been accredited to the fern. It has been prized as the essential ingredient in a love potion, while at the same time feared because it carried the mark of the devil. Right up to the present day it has been a source of folklore and mysticism, as well as an inspiration for poets and painters.

The curious little moonwort, *Botrychium lunaria*, has a long association with fairies and magic. It is an unusual fern which, to quote a 19th century fern admirer, 'grows apart from its kind, on the open face of meadows, under the play of moonbeams'. It was treated with great respect in medieval times, when it earned the names 'blasting roots' and 'spring wurzel', as it was thought to have the power to open locks and unshoe horses that trod in the meadows where it grew. Country people avoided and feared it for its supposed powers over metal, and alchemists prized it for the same reason.

Simple country people believed that fairies used the pinnae of the moonwort to saddle their horses (the pinnae, where they spread out and away from the stem, look just like a saddle) then rode like Queen Mab, who Shakespeare tells us galloped 'night by night through lovers' brains, and then they dream of love' (*Romeo and Juliet*, I, iv).

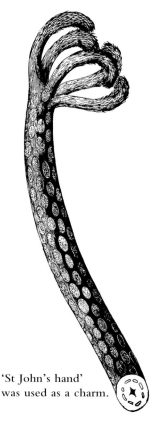

'St John's hand' was used as a charm.

If the fairies on their magical moonwort saddles failed to stir feelings of love, a potion made from *Dryopteris filix-mas* (male fern) may have worked better. This fern was considered an essential ingredient in love potions; if concocted by a witch, chances were that it would be more successful. Put to broader use, the male fern was thought to bring good luck if the dried smoked rhizome was fashioned into the shape of a hand and worn as a charm known as 'St John's hand'. The same powers were attributed to *Athyrium filix-femina* (lady fern); interestingly, this fern was not considered as powerful.

Ferns are mentioned frequently in the *Doctrine of Signature*. This was an ancient belief that related to the interpretation of the shapes and patterns formed when connecting bundles of tissues in roots, stems and leaves are cut horizontally. It was a powerful belief and greatly influenced simple and superstitious people of olden days. The pattern found in the tissues of the bracken *Pteridium aquilinum* formed the letter 'C' and was taken to be Christ's initial. This fern was therefore prized as a protection against

Scythian lamb — travellers to central Europe and Asia in the 1700s brought back stories of a charm in the shape of a lamb. It came from the caudex of *Dicksonia barometz* and was thought to ward off evil. When dried, the long silk hairs resembled wool, and a small piece of rhizome with frond stalks attached did look like a lamb.

witches, goblins and other emissaries of the devil. In Scotland, the letter 'X' was found in the tissues of the same fern. This, being the ancient Greek symbol for Christ, was another good sign. However, there is also a record of the mark of the devil's hoof in the tissues of the roots of the bracken found in Scotland, so it seems that this fern had a rather chequered history in Britain. In parts of England, the bracken has also been known as 'King Charles in the Oak Tree' because the picture depicted in the stem fibres was sometimes thought to be that of the King hiding in a tree to escape his enemies.

The mysterious way in which ferns regenerate caused speculation for centuries. People thought that the 'invisible' seed had the power to impart this quality to its finder. Shakespeare refers to it in *Henry IV* when Chamberlain says to Gadshill, 'You are more beholding to the night than to fern seed for your walking invisible.'

Many pagan ceremonies sprang up around this belief of invisibility. One was to 'catch' the fern seed. At midnight on St John's Eve, 12 pewter plates were placed under the 'black spotted frond' (the black spots were thought to have something to do with seeding and that they fell suddenly on Midsummer Eve). The magical seed, in falling, would pass through 11 of the plates and rest on the 12th. If the gatherers were able to 'catch' the seed on the 12th plate and forestall the fairies who were also present to snatch the seed away, they would possess the coveted quality of invisibility. This superstition existed in Worcestershire, England, amongst country people, as late as the 19th century.

Athyrium filix-femina

CHAPTER 3

CULTIVATION

If you wish to grow ferns successfully, it is necessary to understand them, and helpful to have a close look at the places in which they grow naturally. Although ferns grow in all climatic zones from temperate to tropical, the natural habitat for most species is moist, sheltered from the sun and protected from wind.

In a suitable habitat — a gully or small ravine at the base of a mountain close to the sea — there will be a high canopy of trees, and, under that, another canopy of spreading tree ferns. The trunks of the trees on the side closest to the mountain will be enveloped in aerial ferns, and crevices in the rocky walls of the gully will be filled with tiny lithophytes. Climbing ferns will have found their way to the low-growing branches of the trees and covered them with a soft mantle of green.

On the ground in this lush place, there will be the terrestrial ferns, their roots binding the mass of mouldering leaf litter that clothes the forest floor. Under the ground ferns, there will be tiny new sporophytes and quillworts and mosses; and closer to the damp earth again, a green film formed by the developing prothalli.

The light is dappled, filtering softly through the trees overhead. The air is still. The atmosphere is cool, with vapours rising from the forest floor. The moisture in the air may be so dense that it condenses on overhead fronds and drips constantly onto the earth below. The floor of the forest is covered with a dense mat of fallen leaves, fronds, twigs and bark and, under that, is a denser mat of half-rotted matter. Under that again is a crumbly brown humus that is almost one with the soil. Water that is fresh and clear seeps through the ground, trickles away and is constantly replenished.

These are the ideal conditions in which ferns grow. They can be easily and ingeniously reproduced in glasshouses, shade or green houses, in the open garden and in the house, without too much expense or trouble.

LIGHT REQUIREMENTS

All plants need natural light to manufacture food by the process called *photosynthesis*. Light rays, chiefly the red, blue and violet, are the energy sources that plants use to fuse water and carbon dioxide within the leaf to form the plant's food, sugar. Some plants can carry out this process in a wide range of conditions. Ferns, on the whole, prefer degrees of shade for photosynthesis.

At both ends of this shade scale ferns will probably grow, usually struggling on for a while, for they are adaptable, until they succumb and die. Light that is too strong or full sunshine for a significant part of the day can alter the appearance of a fern. Both fronds and stems become thicker, smaller, less luxuriant and have a yellow tinge. A fern grown in strong light will look much tougher than another of the same species grown in softer light. A fern will adapt to such a situation by altering its appearance; however, if the sunlight becomes too hot and if a harsh drying wind reaches even those tough fronds, and if the roots dry out on such a day, the plant could wilt and die, or at the very least it could suffer a serious setback.

A contrived grotto in a Victorian fernery.

Light that is intensified through a pane of glass can fade a fern. This will often happen with a plant kept by a window inside a house. If it is kept too close to a window that gets direct and strong light for a greater part of the day, the fronds will take on a greyish and translucent quality. Too little light will cause fronds to be elongated and limp.

The older the plant, the more light it requires. The prothallus grows low down on the soil, shaded and protected by the fronds of the parent plant, but needs more light as the true fern develops. When a baby plant is introduced into a collection, it will grow best if sheltered under a bigger plant until it is of comparable size.

Through observation of the colour and general appearance of a fern, it is possible to judge if the fronds are looking dull or pale because of too much light; or if they are elongated because they have been in the dark for too long. The fern's reactions to light intensities are not immediate; a day or two will tell if the light is too strong, and, within a week or two, there will be evidence of insufficient light. You should, though, act immediately if you suspect that light intensities are not correct. Ferns are hardy and do recover from little setbacks, but we should not ask too much of them.

Though all ferns become more demanding when grown indoors, the needs of individual ferns will vary. For example, one may tolerate only a few days near a certain window before it looks a little wan and may need four or five days outside to pick up. Another may tolerate the same situation for much longer. The varying intensity and angle of light through the changing seasons will also affect plants grown indoors, and it may take a fair amount of juggling of spaces and plants, and organising of blinds and reflectors, to keep indoor ferns happy in the same space all the year round.

ATMOSPHERE

A moist atmosphere is essential to ferns' wellbeing. They need at least 30%, but do better at 60–80% relative humidity during the day and at a slightly lower reading at night. This applies to ferns in the house, glasshouse, and shade house or greenhouse. Humidity is the key to successful growing of most ferns as indoor plants.

Low humidity seems to inhibit new growth, causing it to shrivel. Old, established growth yellows or the edges of the leaflets go brown and the whole frond becomes brittle and eventually drops off. Conversely, an excessively high humidity is not necessarily better for ferns. Lower night-time humidity is necessary, not only because it duplicates natural outdoor conditions, but also because it inhibits the growth of moulds.

The various methods of increasing the moisture content of the air are discussed in detail in the chapters to do with keeping plants in the house (pp. 87–88), glasshouse (pp. 84–87), and shade house or greenhouse (p. 83).

AIR

If the air in a room which contains plants seems fresher, it *is* possibly fresher, because plants take up carbon dioxide from the atmosphere (the waste gas that animals exhale from their lungs) and use it in their energy-making process, known as photosynthesis. Photosynthesis results in the release of oxygen into the air. A little carbon dioxide is also

Pellaea falcata

released in the respiration process during the hours of darkness, when photosynthesis stops. Very small amounts of stale gas do not warrant the removal of plants from a room at night, as was so assiduously done in bygone days.

This need for carbon dioxide does not mean that a fern, or any plant for that matter, will thrive in a stale atmosphere; plants need oxygen for respiration in the same way as any living thing. Respiration is carried out in the same cells as is photosynthesis; but, unlike photosynthesis, which is a daytime activity only, respiration is a continual process.

So ferns must have fresh air. Smog, fumes from gas, oil smoke, rooms constantly filled and warmed with body heat (such as restaurants) are destructive over long periods and certainly damaging over short ones.

A sudden change of air introduced through an open window will not always be beneficial; any change to even a cool, airy situation should be gradual. Constant hot or cold draughts, even little ones from under a closed window, will damage delicate fern fronds and new growth will remain stunted on the side that is exposed to the draught. This is a source of damage to be checked if plants appear lopsided.

Blechnum gibbum

A constant but gentle flow of fresh moist air is what is most beneficial to ferns growing in an enclosed atmosphere, such as indoors or in a glasshouse. Gentle little eddies should continually move around and among the fronds, constantly replenishing the life-giving air and moving used gases and dangerous fungus spores.

SOIL

*Soil p*H

Generally ferns prefer an acid soil and grow best at a pH of between 6 and 7; and the majority will not grow in any but acid conditions. (Simple soil testing kits can be bought from nurseries or, if the whole garden is to be tested, your local Department of Agriculture usually provides a service for a small fee.) In their natural state, ferns take root in the spongy layer of leaf mould and humus that has accumulated on the forest floor for centuries. This decayed matter is rich in nitrogen and is on the acid side of the pH scale. However, this does not mean that you should immediately take steps to increase

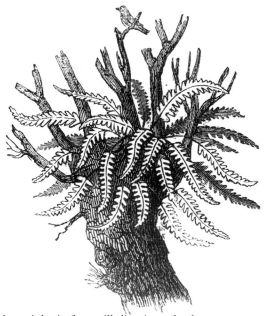

An epiphytic fern will disguise a dead tree stump.

soil acidity. If they are growing well, leave the soil alone; if they are not, check for other adverse conditions first before assuming the soil is not sufficiently acid.

It does not mean, either, that all ferns are not tolerant of lime, for there are many which are native to areas of limestone and grow happily among rocks containing calcium. Many ferns, such as *Cryptogramma crispa* (parsley fern), prefer an acid soil, but will tolerate alkaline soils.

It is much more difficult to increase the acidity of an alkaline soil than it is to increase the alkalinity of an acid soil. It can be done with the application of sulphur, and with the continual application of leaf mould; however, applying sulphur requires care and should be done only after a soil test.

If the soil is too acid, it can be altered by adding lime; however, lime increases the alkalinity, so is not practicable in a fern bed. In this case, gypsum (calcium sulphate) may be added; even though it does not reduce the soil acidity, it is especially useful in the fern bed for reducing stickiness in clay soils and as a general soil conditioner. Rates of application depend on soil types: clay soil needs two and a half times as much gypsum to correct the same degree of acidity as would a sandy soil, so it is best to test the soil first.

Soil Texture

The soil texture, too, is important to successful fern growing. Ferns' roots are delicate, fibrous and shallow, so that they may cling to soft layers of decayed vegetation and obtain the sustenance that they need from this rich organic matter close to the surface; in the sheltered places in which they grow, they do not need a strong root system.

The soil for successful fern growing should similarly be soft and fibrous so that it is moisture retentive; again, similarly, it should be coarse and fairly open so that it will drain readily; and slightly on the acid side of the pH scale.

The structure of the soil may be changed for the better, or conditioned, by using soil additives — organic and inorganic. A soft fibrous texture is obtained by adding organic matter to the soil in the garden; or to the ingredients of a potting mixture in the form of the following: leaf mould (partly decayed leaves); well-decayed garden compost (made without lime); peat moss; wood shavings; sawdust; buzzer chips; finely shredded bark; tree fern fibre (the coarse dust and particles from a chain saw being used on tree fern trunks); very old manure; spent hops; and rice husks. Inorganic substances such as perlite (material from the expansion of siliceous rock), styrofoam beads and vermiculite will also keep a soil mixture in the garden or in a pot soft. Coarse sand (quartz sand and builders' sand which must be washed to prevent it from setting

Many ferns thrive with their roots in damp soil and their fronds overhanging water.

hard); gravel; scoria; crushed rock; and charcoal pieces (which also help to keep the soil sweet through their ability to absorb impurities) are all inorganic, and help to keep the growing medium open, aerated and draining effectively.

In the garden, the soil structure may be altered for fern growing by adding any one, some or all of the substances just mentioned. A closer look at each will explain how it affects the soil.

LEAF MOULD

This organic matter formed by partially decayed leaves is one of the finest soil conditioners for ferns. The best type of leaf mould is considered to be that from oak and beech leaves. When these delicate deciduous leaves are in the process of breaking down, they are rich in many nutrients and have a strong fibrous texture and a crumbly consistency. Leaves from other deciduous trees are not as good as oak and beech for this purpose, but they are better than nothing.

Leaf mould can be gathered from fern gullies, but this is illegal in many parts of the world — what little natural forest we have left is too precious to abuse. Instead, it can be made from the fallen leaves of deciduous street and garden trees. Make a frame of wood, lay light branches and twigs on top of it to form a base that will drain readily, and onto this pile autumn (fall) leaves, layering them with spadefuls of earth. Do not make the heaps more than 1 m (3 ft) high. The leaves will take about one year to break down and form a fibrous mould that is ideal compost for a fern bed.

COMPOST

Compost made from well-decayed garden and kitchen waste can go into a fern bed; however, it should not be used if lime has been added to assist decomposition. A satisfactory compost can also be made from coarse garden waste, such as light prunings, and plants with tough fibrous stalks which take a long time to break down. This coarse material can be kept in an out-of-the-way corner of the garden and left to break down. The resulting compost makes a good conditioner for heavy soil.

PEAT MOSS

This is the ideal organic matter to add to fern beds and potting mixtures as it provides resilience, aeration and water-retentive properties. Peat moss consists of partly or wholly decomposed mosses, such as sphagnum moss. It is sun or kiln dried, and then shredded into various grades. Peat moss contains about twice as much nitrogen as manures; however, it is not in a form that is available to plants and therefore should be regarded as a soil conditioner, not as a fertiliser. It breaks down slowly, keeping the soil loose over a long period of time, and improving the aeration and drainage for that time.

There are various types of peat moss. Avoid the very black type which feels greasy and becomes sticky and adhesive when wet. For ferns, sedge peat should be avoided too, because it does not contain moss and may contain salts. Fine, dusty peat is useless. The best quality is brown peat which is spongy or fibrous; or black peat which has a fluffy texture; both are relatively light.

Peat moss is sometimes sold in such a dehydrated form that it is difficult to handle. It can be better managed by adding water (warm water acts more quickly) through a small opening in the bag, and leaving it to soak through the fibres. This may take a day or two if the bag is big and the peat moss is very dry. This soil conditioner should be evenly moist before you use it. Never mix dry peat moss into a potting mixture — it is almost impossible to mix evenly and, more importantly, it will take up the moisture from the other ingredients and, in the absorption process, will swell and dislodge otherwise firmly potted plants.

Peat moss is expensive and becoming difficult to obtain, so despite its long-lasting qualities, it is not an economical proposition to add to a fern bed. Perhaps you should regard it as a 'luxury' kept for potted plants.

WOOD PRODUCTS

Sawdust, wood chips, buzzer chips, pine bark and wood shavings, and other wood waste products contribute greatly to the structure of soil, but add very few nutrients. In their breaking down process, they can actually rob the soil of some of its nitrogen; this happens when the microorganisms, which convert the wood particles to humus, need mineral nutrients to grow. You should bear this in mind and use these products with care, adding fertiliser to the soil on a regular basis during their decomposition. These products are best used after they have been allowed to decompose for about 12 months. The addition of animal manure hastens the process of decomposition.

Pine bark is a reasonable substitute for peat moss, and an important ingredient in potting mixtures. It is available in various grades. A fine grade with particles of less than 6 mm (¼ in), with at least 40% of a size greater than 1 mm (¹⁄₁₆ in) is ideal for potting mixtures. A coarse grade may be used in the garden and as drainage material in big pots. Pine bark has the same disadvantage as other wood products of taking nitrogen from the soil; however, it does have an advantage in that it breaks down more slowly than wood.

TREE FERN FIBRE

Tree fern fibre, which is the fine, sweet-smelling material resulting from the use of a chain saw on the trunks of tree ferns, makes a very good soil conditioner for all ferns. Like other wood products, it is not decomposed and is best left to break down for 12 months; the resulting humus may then be used as a soil conditioner. It has the advantage of containing a range of fibres: the dense particles of the centre wood and the fine strands and soft tissues which make up the outer layers of the trunk.

It is difficult to obtain, and I can only suggest that you find a nursery which carries a range of containers made of tree fern wood and request the

Cyathea cooperi

owner to order a bag of tree fern fibre from the nursery's supplier. Do make sure that the supplier is a reputable one — it would be a pity to support indirectly someone who is illegally taking these ferns from the world's forests. Osmunda fibre is available in North America. It has a stronger texture than tree fern fibre and makes an ideal growing medium for ferns.

SEAWEED

Seaweed mulch, once it has broken down, makes an excellent soil conditioner. It is rich in nitrogen in a readily available form, providing nearly as much nitrogen and up to three times as much as potash as an equivalent dressing of cow manure. However, it must be thoroughly washed before using on a fern bed. If used for too long, it will increase the alkalinity of the soil.

MANURE

Manure should be used more for its humus content than as a top dressing. It should be old and thoroughly decomposed as it can generate a great deal of heat as it breaks down, and will burn roots and trunks that it contacts. Manure should not be used in conditions where the humidity is high, as it encourages the growth of bacteria and mould.

HOPS AND OTHER CEREALS

Spent hops may be obtained from breweries, and are useful for improving the condition of the soil; however, they are very low in nutrients. The same is true of rice and oat husks.

SAND

One-third of a good standard potting mix should consist of coarse river sand. Sand improves the aeration and drainage in both the garden bed and a pot. It is important that sand *not* be omitted from the potting mixture for strong-growing ferns that you plan to keep in the same pot for several years; it will counter the compression caused by the expanding root system.

If a heavy loam is added to a potting mixture, a coarse grade of sand is recommended. If the loam is already very sandy, the sand may be omitted altogether. Unwashed builders' sand sets hard after it has been wetted and worked, so it is best to avoid it. Sand from the beach should also be avoided, unless washed thoroughly.

VERMICULITE

Vermiculite is a mineral, mica, which has been heated at a high temperature until it expands and becomes sponge-like and capable of absorbing eight times its weight of

A group of *Dicksonia antarctica* after a snow storm, Mt Wellington, Tasmania, Australia.

water. The intense heat used in its preparation leaves it sterile. Its sponge-like quality makes it ideal as a water-retentive material, and it contains a little potassium and calcium in a form available to plants. Its surface provides a favourable site for the movement of minerals within the soil mix. Vermiculite is not a long-term soil conditioner as it breaks down easily.

SCORIA
Scoria is now used frequently in potting mixes, and is suitable as a medium for growing ferns. However, plants will not grow in a potting mixture that is made up solely of scoria, but when scoria is mixed with nutrients, it makes a good substitute for soil and sand. Because of its high pH level, problems such as iron deficiency may develop with prolonged use.

PERLITE

Perlite does not break down as readily as vermiculite. It is a sterile, inorganic material which comes from vitreous rock that has been broken up by clusters of minute spherical cracks. Perlite can be added to soil and soil mixes to provide aeration.

BROWN COAL

Brown coal is useful as a soil additive when combined with other materials. It is also useful as a substitute for soil when used on its own. Its main disadvantage is that is does not form a good mixture with soil because it tends to waterlog easily. On the other hand, it mixes and binds well with other types of materials.

New growth (platelets or pups) on *Platycerium superbum*.

Suggested mixtures to use are one part by volume of brown coal with one part of coarse sand or scoria; or one part of brown coal with one part of pine bark or peat moss. Brown coal has a pH of 6.0 to 6.5, which makes it ideal for ferns, given that they grow best at a pH of between 6.0 and 7.0. Follow-up fertiliser is recommended.

CHARCOAL

Charcoal is a form of carbon, and is a black porous substance made by partially burning wood, bones and animal or vegetable waste. Mixed through soil, it acts as a filter, constantly absorbing toxic materials that accumulate as a result of watering. If waterlogging is suspected to be a problem, whether in the ground or in a pot, charcoal will counteract this.

WATERING

Ferns should be watered when they need it, and must never be allowed to wilt.

There are a few guidelines and many factors to consider. The soil around the roots of most ferns, in the ground or in the pot, must be kept moist. There is a great deal of difference between wet and moist. 'Moist' is an even dampness throughout the soil; 'wet' is a state of constant sogginess that excludes oxygen from the soil. In a wet state, the bacteria in the soil die and the soil becomes a sour-smelling and slimy mass. Ferns require more water than most other house plants growing under similar conditions. However, it should be kept in mind that ferns will need less watering during cool weather, when evaporation from the soil and moisture loss through the leaves is less; and more frequent watering when the weather is warm, and the accompanying, usually drier atmosphere extracts moisture from the soil.

Both the size and make-up of a container in which a plant is growing also affect watering requirements. A plant growing in a small pot will have to be watered more often than one growing in a large pot. A plant growing in a plastic or glazed pot will not need as much water as one growing in an unglazed earthenware container, as a considerable amount of moisture is lost through the sides of an earthenware pot. However, it should also be noted that a clay pot will hold more moisture than a plastic pot as it retains moisture within its walls. (The advantages and disadvantages of plastic and clay pots are discussed in the chapter on container growing, on p. 96.)

The potting mixture in which a plant is growing must also be taken into consideration. A mixture containing heavy loam and dense peat moss or leaf mould will retain moisture longer than a mixture that contains large fibre particles and coarse sand; however, the mixture that retains moisture can readily become waterlogged if not watered carefully.

When to Water

A fern should be watered when the moisture level is getting low for that particular plant's needs. This is indicated by the look and feel of the soil. An initial glance may tell you that the soil is dry, but this is not a true guide. The surface may be dry, but a little below the surface the soil may feel cool and damp. You can test this with your finger.

Moisture meters are useful, but rather expensive, indicators of the amount of moisture in the soil; if you have many potted plants they may be a worthwhile investment. There are cheaper alternatives: condensation on the underside of a small flat pebble placed on the soil indicates the presence of moisture; or you may simply judge if a plant needs watering by the feel of the pot. A pot that is dry will feel light in comparison to one that has just been watered. This will be difficult to assess if the plants are in big pots, so you can employ the 'sound' technique instead. If the soil is dry, the pot will make a sharp ringing sound when tapped lightly on its side; one that contains plenty of moisture will sound dull. This technique works well for terracotta pots.

How to Water

POTTED PLANTS

Both potted ferns and those growing in the garden require thorough soaking. Potted plants should be watered until water flows freely through the drain holes. Thorough watering ensures that the moisture is distributed throughout the soil and the root ball itself. Thorough watering also flushes out the salts, which may be present owing to frequent tap watering. These salts are visible as a grey crystalline crust on the surface of the soil; they should be scraped off and the soil flushed. Always apply a gentle water pressure through the fine nozzle of the hose; hard direct pressure will dislodge soil particles from around the roots of small-growing ferns.

Potted plants are easier to water if the plant has been potted so that the soil is at least 2 cm (1 in) below the rim.

Small potted plants may be soaked in a tub of water. This is an effective way of wetting a potting mixture that has dehydrated completely. Some commercial mixtures may contain a great deal of fibre and inorganic materials that are very hard to reconstitute; and exceptionally light mixtures will float away if submerged. The best way to cope with this is to anticipate the problem and weigh the soil down with a cloth or stones.

However, it is not good for the fern to be left to soak too long; it should soak only long enough to ensure that the soil is wet through. If left too long, the water may become chilled and the roots may be deprived of oxygen.

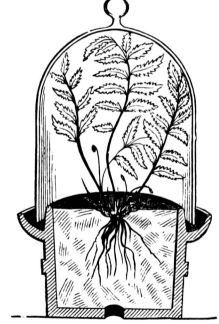

The principle of the Victorian 'closed case' — the lip around the pot contains water, thus excluding air once the glass shade is in place.

IN THE GARDEN

In the garden, deep watering is essential to encourage roots to grow deeply, anchor themselves firmly and take advantage of a larger area for food. Frequent light watering encourages roots to stay near the soil surface, where they are vulnerable to drying out if a day's watering is missed; and to damage from cultivation and the digging of cats and dogs.

Warnings

Fern fronds should not be wetted and allowed to stay wet. Fronds that are wet and standing in the sunlight may develop dark burn spots where the droplets of water have intensified the burning effect of the sun's rays. Foliage should not stay wet overnight in the cold weather as it may freeze; nor should it be wet for any length of time in a humid atmosphere as this may bring on fungal and bacterial growths.

Water should not be poured into the centre of the crown of a fern that develops a trunk, such as a tree fern; if wet for too long, the soft woody tissue in the centre of the caudex will rot and new fronds will not develop.

Effective drainage is essential to a potted fern. After watering, make sure that the water is flowing freely out of the drain holes in the pot. The flow of water may be aided by standing the pot on a rack; or on sand or pebbles in a tray. If the pot stands in a saucer, make sure that water that drains away does not accumulate in the saucer. Toxic salts build up in the soil of a potted plant and should be washed away with thorough watering. For this reason, water that accumulates in a saucer should never be tipped back over a plant.

Where ferns grow naturally, the ground is always wet, but the water is constantly moving and being replenished by fresh water. In the garden, effective drainage is also essential; otherwise, accumulated water will become stagnant and roots will rot.

Rain

The most effective watering for potted ferns is light showers of rain, which will gently and thoroughly wash their fronds free of garden and house dust, and flush toxic salts from the soil. Of course, the rain must be gentle and unaccompanied by wind or hail.

Water Temperature

Rainwater is usually warm, and is beneficial to a fern that has been growing in mild conditions, like those in a glasshouse or inside a house. Water that is approximately the same temperature as the fern's surroundings should be used when hand watering, or soaking plants. This can be done by standing the watering can in the same room as the ferns for a while so that the water is the same temperature as the room. Some growers believe that this also allows any chemicals in tap water to settle, or evaporate. Water temperature should range from 18°C (65°F) to 26°C (80°F) — the water should feel comfortable to touch. A sudden rush of cold water through the soil can damage roots and retard growth. The hot water from hoses left lying in the sun can also be damaging.

PLANTING AND TRANSPLANTING

When any plant is moved from the place or pot in which it is growing, it may be damaged, no matter how carefully handled; inevitably, some roots are lost and the delicate root hairs, which are the plant's feeding systems, are dislodged or bruised. The plant must replace these, repair damaged tissues, re-anchor itself and adjust to new surroundings, so moving day should be made as easy on the plant as possible.

Hardening

Potted plants can be prepared for transfer to the garden bed by being left to stand for a few days in the area in which they are to be planted. This gives the foliage time to adjust gradually to new light and air conditions. Plants bought from nurseries these days are rarely 'hardened' before sale as they once were. Commercial growers used to maintain a 'hardening house' where plants were kept for a week or so to give them time to adjust to outside conditions; only conscientious growers do this now. Most are hard-pressed to keep up with the demand for potted house plants which are, more often than not, regarded as disposable ornaments by people who cannot be bothered with their care. Many failures with potted house plants, and ferns in particular, are due to this neglect.

When buying a new plant, be sure that your nursery deals with a reputable grower, or at least be aware that the plants they buy may not be 'hardened'. Also be sure that the plant you have selected from a nursery has not been kept in the dark, or in full sun, or in a draughty or exposed place.

Planting

FERNS WITH CREEPING RHIZOMES
This includes plants such as the *Polypodium* and *Davallia* genera, which should be planted so that the rhizome rests lightly on the soil and the fibrous roots are firmly and completely covered. The tip should point in the direction you wish it to take.

FERNS WITH ERECT RHIZOMES

Ferns such as the *Asplenium* and *Blechnum* genera are caudescent (i.e. form a caudex or pseudo-trunk). They should have old, dead parts of the caudex pared away with a sharp knife until living tissue is exposed, then planted so that the crown is level with the soil surface. Unless they are pared in this way, the tissues will not be stimulated to produce new growth.

YOUNG, SOFT-TISSUED FERNS

Young, soft-tissued ferns should be planted so that the original soil level is maintained. Any lower, the stems will rot; any higher, that area of the root zone above the ground will not be able to function.

EPIPHYTIC FERNS

The care of epiphytic ferns is very similar to that for terrestrial ferns; however, extra attention must be paid to the drainage of the medium in which the plant grows, whether it is in the ground or in a pot. Bear in mind that an epiphyte grows naturally on another plant, usually fairly high on a tree or on another tall-growing fern. Under these conditions, the roots function in the accumulated humus in the bark, fibre or crevices of the host plant. This humus is never wet for any length of time — in fact, it can become quite dry in between rainfalls. Thus, the soil in which an epiphyte grows should drain well; or agricultural drains should be installed, or the plant moved to higher ground. In a pot, extra grit in the potting mix, and an extra layer of crocks in the bottom, will permit the water to drain away

Platycerium wandae

quickly. Watering of a fern that is a lithophyte or an epiphyte should be done when the soil is on the dry side of moist.

Clay and wooden pots with large drain holes, and wooden or wire baskets lined with natural materials such as bark or moss, are better for epiphytic ferns than plastic pots. These materials are porous and allow the air to circulate through the potting mixture and the roots, so the plant is growing close to its natural state.

Transplanting

A fern's dormant time is *not* the time to move it: it must be actively growing during early spring or late autumn (fall). In temperate areas, if midsummer conditions are prevailingly dry, planting should be delayed. In tropical areas, if growth has not stopped, a fern may be moved at any time.

POTTED PLANTS AND SMALLER FERNS

A potted plant should be watered the day before planting as it is easier to remove from the pot when damp; and there is less likelihood of soil coming away from the root ball and taking tiny roots and root hairs with it. If large, fibrous roots have been broken while being transferred, they should be cut off cleanly with a sharp knife or secateurs, and a complementary amount of top growth removed as near to the crown as possible.

Gymnocarpium dryopteris

LARGER FERNS

Before lifting a big fern that is likely to have a dense root ball, leave the hose running on it gently to soak it thoroughly for several hours; it is easier, and safer, to remove when the soil is damp. A very large fern, such as a tree fern, should have a trench dug around it 45 cm (18 in) from the trunk. It should then be left as long as possible — preferably for the whole growing season before you intend to move it — so that it can make new roots close to the trunk. This is best carried out in early spring while growth is at its peak. The trench should be dug with a sharp spade that severs the roots cleanly to a depth of at least 30 cm (12 in). Fill this trench with loose fibrous material and grit to encourage new root development at this point, so that, when the plant is moved, new roots have already formed and are ready to spread out into the new ground. (This is not necessary for *Dicksonia antarctica* (soft tree fern), which may be transplanted easily when the trunk is sawn through at any point; however, it is a very useful method if the height of the fern is to be retained.)

FERTILISERS

There is a theory that fertilising a fern accelerates its growth and shortens its life. A handful of old cow manure, blood and bone or leaf mould, while ferns are growing in spring and summer, should be all that they need. Ferns require plenty of nitrogen. If a commercial chemical fertiliser is used as a nitrogen supplement, it should be 'complete', or 'balanced'. Pure chemicals, such as sulphate or ammonia, will upset the balance of the soil chemistry, which will take a long time to rectify. Nitrogen in the form of organic hoof and horn meal can be freely used in a garden bed, but the equivalent amount administered in the form of an inorganic fertiliser, such as nitrate of soda, would be damaging. A 'complete' fertiliser is one that contains the three main plant foods: nitrogen (N), phosphorus (P) and potash (K); an 'incomplete' fertiliser is one that contains only one, or two, of these foods. Both fertilisers are available in organic and inorganic, liquid and dry forms. Some are fast release, some are slow release. All commercially made fertilisers must carry an analysis of their contents on the container, so that it is possible to assess how 'complete' or balanced a particular product may be. Commercial products advertised as having 'low burn' properties are recommended for ferns because these fertilisers contain fewer soluble salts.

Use all chemical fertilisers with care and follow the instructions on the packet; the recommended amounts can be halved if you are in doubt — a good practice when feeding soft-tissued ferns.

Organic Fertilisers

Organic fertilisers are of animal or vegetable origin; often derived from slaughter houses, refuse and vegetable wastes such as seed residues. They contain mainly nitrogen in the form of protein, which soil organisms change into nitrates for plants' use. Animal wastes often contain bone residue which provides phosphates; some also contain potash, as well as some trace elements. (Trace elements are the minor foods that all plants need in small quantities.)

Organic fertilisers may be given in the form of blood and bone, hoof and horn meal, fish meal, castor meal and wood ashes. Leaf mould, compost and manure — also excellent natural fertilisers — have been discussed already; they act more as soil conditioners than food supplements. Leaf mould is the most balanced, being both an ideal fertiliser and an ideal soil conditioner.

BLOOD AND BONE

Blood and bone is processed meat meal. It contains 5–6% nitrogen and 10–14% phosphoric acid and is often confused with dried blood and bone dust fertilisers. Both are suited to fern culture. If the soil is warm, dried blood has a fast, sustained fertilising effect; bone dust supplies a slow and steady flow of nutrients depending on the grade of the particles. Dried blood, however, contains many soluble salts and should be used carefully for ferns.

HOOF AND HORN

Hoof and Horn is useful in potting mixtures because of its coarse texture. Its 12% nitrogen content is readily available to plants and has a long-lasting effect.

FISH MEAL

Fish meal (5–10% nitrogen, 2–6% phosphoric acid) usually consists of fish wastes combined with inorganic fertilisers. It acts quickly, giving a sustained supply of nitrogen and phosphorus, but should not be used as a sole and continual food supplement for ferns as it builds up alkalis in the soil. Fish manures are balanced fertilisers — all the major foods are contained in them in balanced proportions.

WOOD ASH

Wood ash is a rich source of potash, but wood ashes vary according to the materials burnt. Hardwood is the greatest source. However, too great a build-up of ashes in the soil of a fern bed makes it too alkaline for most plants' needs.

Inorganic Fertilisers

Inorganic fertilisers derived from chemicals or mining processes provide a concentrated food until leached from the soil. They must be applied with care, or the effects will be felt too quickly and for only a brief period. Frequent applications of chemical fertilisers will promote luxuriant top growth, but the root system will not develop accordingly. If the fertiliser is withdrawn, the plant will not be able to support itself.

Inorganic fertilisers are available in dry, liquid, tablet and slow-release granule forms. Concentrates in small bottles, tablets wrapped in individual plastic containers, and dry forms in elaborate dispensers are expensive but they are also very convenient. Bulk liquids and dry fertilisers are cheaper; however, be sure that you can use them all within the prescribed time as some fertilisers change in composition if they are kept for very long periods, or deteriorate significantly in quality. Check with the manufacturer before you invest in bulk supplies.

Liquid, tablet and slow-release granules are easily measured. Liquids are distributed evenly through the soil with less likelihood of an accidental overdose burning foliage and roots; but there is considerable waste in run-off and bypassing of the root zone.

Tablets should be used with caution. Because ferns are watered more frequently than most other plants, the tablets may disperse more quickly than manufacturers anticipate, and roots may be damaged by a concentration of chemicals.

Dry inorganic fertiliser should be spread evenly over the soil — it can be mixed with soil before spreading to make distribution easier — and it should be kept away from the fronds of the ferns. It is also equally important to ensure that no fertiliser falls into the crown of a fern during application, because it may burn the embryonic crosiers. The dry fertilisers require rather more care in their application, but they are cheap in comparison to liquid fertilisers, and they last longer.

A covering of frost over ferns on a winter's morning.

Words of Warning about Fertilisers

After using fertilisers, new growth must be watched carefully. This tender part of the plant can be burned by the fertiliser which, at the same time, can cause established growth to appear to flourish. If new growth is continually burned away by fertiliser that is too strong, or is applied too frequently, the plant will die. This may be the reason for the death of a plant that until, and for some time after, the application of fertiliser, seemed to be thriving.

When a fern is not thriving, do not automatically fertilise it. Look for other possible problems such as waterlogged soil, poor ventilation or insufficient light.

If a plant has been damaged due to fertiliser, the leaves go brittle and brown. Careful repotting, so that the plant does not suffer yet another setback, may help it to recover. Old ferns with woody roots and trunks may be able to recover from an overdose of fertiliser; young plants probably cannot.

It is a waste of time and fertiliser to feed a fern that is dormant.

YEAR-ROUND MANAGEMENT

Spring

In spring, when ferns begin to grow again, they need more water and a new mulch of leaf mould or old cow manure. Fronds that have grown early in spring may need protection from sudden hot or cold winds that capricious spring can bring. Old fronds that threaten to crowd and distort emerging new growth should be cut away.

Aphids and people are a fern's worst spring enemies. Both can damage new fronds that will remain that way, spoiling the appearance of the plant for several seasons, until they are replaced. Look for aphids, which may be difficult to detect amidst the profuse new growth, and destroy them; and discourage people from touching the tender new crosiers as they unfurl.

Summer

In summer, ferns need protection from strong sunlight and hot winds. Those that have been growing in gentle spring sunlight may have to be moved to a shadier position. Those in hanging baskets should be protected from the dehydrating effects of hot winds, and from heat reflected off any metal surroundings which may burn the fronds. On very hot days, sun beating on the sides of pots can make them hot and roots may be scorched.

Baskets and pots which have been placed under a tree for protection from the sun will need attention to their water needs, even after rain, as trees can act as giant umbrellas.

Ferns need deep mulches at this time of year to keep their roots cool and to cut down moisture loss through evaporation; but mulches should be kept away from stems and rhizomes in a humid atmosphere, as this may encourage fungal growth.

Autumn (Fall)

New fronds may continue to appear until early autumn (fall), but later, growth will slow down and ferns of the temperate areas will become dormant. Ferns that retain fronds should not be pruned as removal may encourage new growth that is not sufficiently hardy to withstand low winter temperatures. The old fronds will also protect the past season's growth should the fern be in an exposed place over winter.

Ferns do not need feeding at this time of the year and watering should be reduced to a minimum. Old mulch should be left in place because spores may have fallen. If you look closely you may find tiny green prothalli forming on its surface.

Winter

Most ferns will survive the winter months with little care. Deciduous varieties remain dormant requiring only to be left alone and for their soil to be kept on the dry side of moist. Semi-deciduous ferns, and those from the temperate areas which have been growing in colder places, require protection from frost; and to be tolerated while they are not looking their best.

Hymenophylloides

CHAPTER 4

PROPAGATION
AND HYBRIDISING

PROPAGATION

The propagation of ferns is a slow, but interesting, process, and an economical method of increasing a collection.

New ferns can be raised in two ways — by vegetative means or by spores. Vegetative methods are carried out by division. planting or layering of bulbils, auricle cuttings, meristem culture and apospory or apogamy. Each method is explained in detail in the following.

Many ferns are easily propagated by division; it is the only way in which some cultivars may be increased because many of them are sterile or do not grow true to type from spores. Ferns that form creeping surface rhizomes or root stocks, such as the *Davallia* and *Polypodium* genera, can be cut up cleanly — not broken or torn — into portions 5–8 cm (2–3 in) long. Dead tissue should be cut away; damaged roots trimmed; old and excess fronds removed; and the portions replanted at their original level in a potting mixture that contains a high proportion of fibre and grit.

Cut portions of the rhizome of epiphyte ferns, such as some of the *Asplenium* species, should be placed in sphagnum moss and leaf mould rather than in a mixture containing soil, as it is closer to the natural growing medium.

Plants that form crowns, such as the *Blechnum* and *Polystichum* genera, can be propagated by the vegetative method. Strong-growing crowns should be removed by separating them from the mother plant with a sharp knife, ensuring that each plantlet has sufficient living tissue and roots to survive. The new plants can then be placed in a well-drained potting mixture in a pot just big enough to contain their roots.

Layering Bulbils

Plants that form colonies in their natural habitat, like the *Asplenium bulbiferum* (mother or hen and chicken fern), *Polystichum proliferum* (mother shield fern) and *Woodwardia radicans* (European chain fern), often grow a great many plantlets or bulbils on their fronds along the rachis (midrib) or on the tip of the frond. They appear first as small scaly knobs, then as embryonic fronds which, as the parent frond matures, are forced down gradually into closer contact with the soil. Upon contact with the soil, roots develop and the miniature plant, a true sporophyte, is ready for independent growth.

To encourage growth, the mature bulbil-bearing frond may be pegged onto a damp propagating mix in a pot or seedling box until independent growth is obvious. The frond may then be separated from the parent plant and allowed to rot away. Alternatively, the larger bulbils may be snipped off, with a small portion of the parent frond, and planted.

Bulbil production of another kind can sometimes be encouraged in an old plant of *Asplenium scolopendrium* (hart's-tongue fern) where the frond base remains green and fleshy long after — in some instances it may be years after — the fronds have withered. The old fronds can be pulled away from the main trunk of the plant, trimmed of any dead matter and laid firmly in propagating mixture in a pot or a seedling box. After a few weeks, these fronds may produce up to a dozen white bulbils which can be removed and planted. The remains of the stock plant can then be trimmed of dead tissue and replanted lower down in the soil, with a few fronds being left at the top of the plant. This may sometimes have the effect of rejuvenating an old plant.

Bulbils or plantlets growing on a frond of *Asplenium bulbiferum*.

Offsets and Auricle Tips

Offsets are formed by some of the tree-like ferns of the *Blechnum*, *Dicksonia* and *Cyathea* genera; new plants can be propagated from them. Remove the offset from the parent plant with a sharp knife, taking an almost equal amount of the parent tissue with it, and plant in a potting mix that contains a high proportion of sharp sand to stimulate the tissue to produce roots. As it is essential to keep these offsets moist, use a glass cloche or clear plastic cover to prevent dehydration. New plants are often very slow to start.

Two genera, *Angiopteris* and *Marattia*, produce fleshy ear-like protuberances on the rhizome below the stipe or stem base. These can be cut away and planted so that the *auricle tip* is just above the soil. In time, one, sometimes two, new plants may develop.

Meristem Culture

Meristem culture, or tissue culture, involves autoclaves and laboratory-like equipment, and should be left to commercial growers who produce large numbers of plants. Orchids and ferns are being mass-produced in this way. The process is revolutionising wholesale growing and in some instances where plants, such as those in the *Nephrolepis* genus, are particularly suited to this propagation method, spore-raising houses are being phased out.

A tiny piece of tissue is removed from a mature stock plant, sterilised, placed in a growth stimulating and maintaining solution and sealed in a flask. As new growths are produced, they are separated from the parent tissue and placed in larger sealed containers. When growth is about 2 cm (1 in) high — after about three months — the *mericlone* is placed in seedling boxes and cared for in the open glasshouse. As the tissue is removed from adult plants and the cells are matured chemically, it grows twice as fast as seedling plants and within a year the mericlone has the appearance of an advanced plant. However, buyers must be aware that they are buying forced plants, used to hothouse treatment and probably not hardened in the old-fashioned nursery grower's way.

Apospory and Apogamy

Some ferns and fern varieties, such as *Polystichum setiferum* var. *pulcherrimum*, reproduce through non-sexual methods called apospory and apogamy.

Apospory development occurs directly from a deformed spore capsule; or directly from a frond or pinna, rather like a bulbil. This is a first generation prothallus, *not* a second generation sporophyte.

Apogamy development occurs from a bud on the prothallus without sexual fertilisation occurring within the prothallus. *Pteris cretica* (Cretan or ribbon brake) and *Cyrtomium falcatum* (house or Japanese holly fern) are examples of ferns that can develop in this way. Growth of this type results from a spore that is self-fertile, i.e. a spore that contains the requisite number of chromosomes.

Growth from both apospory and apogamy development can be cultivated by pegging the frond bearing the growth down onto a propagating mix that has been dampened. The surrounding atmosphere must be kept warm and moist.

Vegetative propagation methods are best carried out in the warmer months of the year when the plants are growing strongly. The forming, or newly formed, plants should be kept under glass and if possible, with what growers call 'bottom heat' — i.e. heated soil — until well established.

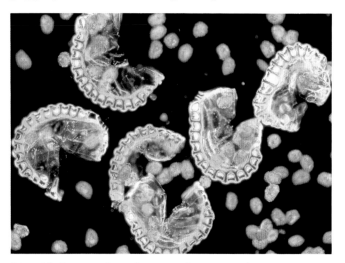
Magnified sporangia and spores of *Dryopteris filix-mas*.

Success with any method of propagation is more likely if attention is paid to sterile potting mixtures, clean pots, high and constant humidity, filtered light and gentle handling of new plants.

Spore Culture

Spore culture is simple. However, there are a few procedures which must be carried out with care to avoid disappointments.

Containers, soil mixtures and utensils should be scrupulously clean. Only pure rainwater or boiled water should be used, and every procedure should be carried out without delay. These precautions are necessary to exclude the growth of algae, fungi, liverworts and mosses that thrive in the same conditions as the prothalli; and which can overwhelm delicate prothallial growth.

There are several methods of spore raising, but the following is a fairly simple and traditional method. From midsummer onwards, the spores are collected from a mature frond which still holds sporangia that appear to be ripe. You may need a magnifying glass to see this. Check that all the sporangia are still intact; and have not opened and already shed their spores. Spore cases will have a ragged look if they have already opened.

Collect the spore by snipping off a suitable piece of frond, laying it between folded clean white paper, and keep it in a warm, dry place. After a few days, the sporangia will have opened and shed their spores, which appear as fine dust on the paper. The spores are then gently tapped onto a smaller piece of paper which is folded, as a protection, until sowing starts.

The sooner the spores are sown, the better will be the results. The viable period of spores varies greatly. Some, like the spores of the *Osmunda* genus, lose their viability within days. Others, like the spores of the *Todea* and *Leptopteris* genera, lose their viability within hours. Though the spores of most other genera remain viable for a longer time, even for years, it is better to sow as quickly as possible.

Different formations of sori found on the backs of fertile fronds.

STERILISING EQUIPMENT

Shallow pans or pots of terracotta or plastic should be thoroughly cleaned and scalded with boiling water before used. Pots are then filled, first with a layer of drainage material and then chopped sphagnum moss, peat moss, tree fern fibre or commercial seed raising mixture. This should be sterilised by pouring boiling water over it. A piece of netting or muslin over the top of the pot will stop the mixture from flooding over the sides while the water is being poured. After sterilisation, the pot should immediately be covered with a sheet of glass or plastic film (cling wrap), so that uninvited fungi and moss spores do not settle on it.

When the growing medium has cooled the spores are spread as evenly as possible over the surface, and then covered quickly with glass or plastic. Spores are easier to spread if they are mixed with washed fine sand.

WATERING

The pot is plunged into a container of clean water and the growing medium thoroughly dampened, then drained. Boiled or rainwater should again be used, and the medium kept on the wet side of moist. The cover is left on the pot until embryonic fronds appear; if removed earlier, it could permit the entry of unwanted organisms.

The pots containing spores should be placed in a shady, protected situation. From four weeks to six months later, a fine green 'scum' formed by the developing prothalli will become evident. Several weeks after these first visible signs of growth, the prothalli's distinctive heart shape will be obvious; and a few weeks later the first true embryonic fronds will appear.

At this stage, the cover may be removed from the pot and the plants gradually hardened; and pricked out if they are big enough to handle. 'Pricking out' means lifting, separating and spacing individual plants — a tedious and time-consuming job, but necessary if the plants are to develop well. Pricking out will be difficult if the spores have not been sown evenly. It requires a steady hand and patience, but the tiny plants will tolerate a fair amount of handling if the roots do not dry out.

It may take as long as two years before new plants are ready to go into 10-cm (4-in) pots. By that time, a few mature fronds should have formed and the root ball developed to a stage where it almost fills the pot.

Another simple and conventional sowing method is to fill a sterilised terracotta pot with sphagnum moss and invert it in a saucer of water. Spores are sown in the base of the pot, which is then covered with a glass cloche. A brick standing in water and covered by a glass cloche can be used similarly, but should first be sterilised with boiling water to kill any unwanted spores.

HYBRIDISING

Hybridisation does not often happen in nature. There are two propagation methods to achieve hybridisation of ferns: one is a simple 'hit and miss' method, the other more scientific. Neither method is beyond the expertise of the average fern grower.

The first method involves sowing a thick mixture of spores of two species in the same shallow straight-sided pan. The pan is then doused daily with a fine jet of water for several days, when the prothalli are at the fertilisation stage. Alternatively, the prothalli may be just submerged in lukewarm water, and the water gently swirled around the pan several times a day, for two or three days. It must be done as frequently as this as the sexual organs of each species may mature on different days.

Inspection through a microscope is necessary in order to determine if the prothalli are mature enough to release sperm — a magnifying glass is not powerful enough. The male organs (antheridia) and the female organs (archegonia) are situated in different parts of the prothallus — the archegonia at the notch in the heart-shaped organism and the antheridia on the lower, or basal, part of the plant. The neck of the archegonium opens when the egg cells are ready to be fertilised and a sperm-activating substance, malic acid, is released.

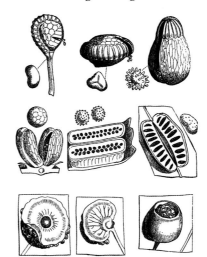

Woodcut of a fern's sexual organs.

The second, more scientific, approach to hybridisation involves some surgery. The spores of the two ferns to be crossed are sown in separate pans, and when the prothalli are ready to be fertilised, the male parts are cut away with a razor blade or scalpel from each prothallus and transferred to the other pan, and placed close to, or overlapping, the female portions of the prothalli. The soil should be kept saturated with water for several days.

Generally, the spores from hybrid plants are sterile and any propagation is done by vegetative methods.

The prothallus, antheridium and archegonium of *Dryopteris filix-mas*.

CHAPTER 5

PESTS AND DISEASES

Several insect pests and a few diseases cause problems with ferns. However, a fern that is not thriving may not necessarily be suffering from disease or an attack by insect pests. More common causes are: waterlogged soil; soil that is dry and cracked, and will not absorb water; hot or cold draughts; too moist or too dry an atmosphere; the plant may be root bound; or it may be in a pot that is too large for it. Check that these are not problems before resorting to a pesticide or fungicide. As prevention is the best means of control, you should discourage people from handling soft new growth and establish a regular maintenance routine which involves a close look under fronds, along the stems and in the axis where stem meets frond, and at soil level; these are places where insect pests are most likely to be found. On the whole, insect pests are responsible for discoloration and lack of vigour in established growth and distortion of new growth so that, with experience, the overall appearance of a plant should give you an indication of any insect pest activity. If you do find such indicators, act promptly, and spray only the affected plant; and keep an eye on it for some time thereafter in case the spray has not been effective. Do not demand total eradication of the pest; perhaps it is better to sacrifice the plant, rather than kill helpful predators and so upset a reasonably balanced garden ecology.

PESTS

Ants

Ants themselves do not damage ferns; however, they are associated with sap-sucking insects like scale, aphids, white flies and mealy bugs, which they guard against predators and nurture for their honeydew secretions. (Honeydew is a heavy sugary solution secreted by sap-sucking insects.) Sooty mould, which is a fungus, frequently grows on heavy deposits of honey dew, thus disguising the insect; the mould itself, if sufficiently heavy, will exclude light from fronds and so compound the problem. Ants, in their farming activities, actually carry baby insects from one plant to another, so that a new plant introduced to an infected collection will quickly become infected too. Ants can be discouraged on a large fern by placing a greasy or sticky band around the trunk — a sticky substance can be made by boiling together 60 ml (2 fl oz) of castor oil and 150 g (5 oz) of resin. Ferns in pots can be protected by placing a greasy or sticky band around the rim of the pot; or by placing the pot on a rack, on a water- or oil-filled saucer. Extra humus added to the soil in the garden bed and to potting mixtures will frustrate the ants' tunnelling activities.

Leaf Hoppers

The passion-vine leaf hopper, which usually feeds on the passionfruit vine, is a fern pest. Viewed from the side, it is a triangular-shaped greenish-brown insect with transparent wings. Both adult and juvenile insects cause distortion of new growth and dead, papery patches on pinnae. It does not present a problem to garden plants, but in the shade house (greenhouse) or glasshouse, where it is free from natural predators, it may cause damage and be difficult to control because it is very mobile. If control is necessary, systemic sprays are known to be effective; or pyrethrum or nicotine sprays. (Matasystox and disulfoton are examples of systemic pesticides — they enter the sap stream through the leaves and foliage, and are distributed throughout the plant. They are readily absorbed through the skin and care should be taken in their use. They are not persistent poisons and break down in a few days.)

Leaf hopper

Eel Worms

Eel worms (*Aphelenchoides fragariae*) are microscopic nematodes which penetrate the frond surface and feed internally. They feed during the cooler months and their presence may be revealed by reddish-brown and black patches between large veins where tissues have collapsed and the veins have impeded the worms' progress. They are difficult to eradicate because rain and routine watering spread the infestations. An affected plant should be quickly isolated and, preferably, destroyed. If the plant is a valuable one, you may try a recommendation of some growers, and steep the fern — if it is a hardy variety — in hot water (about 43°C (110°F)) for 10–15 minutes. Since eel worms do not live in the soil, fumigation of the soil and resort to highly toxic nematicides is not necessary.

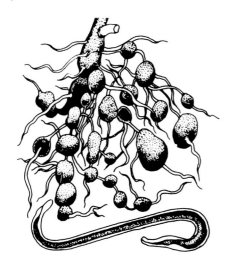

Eel worm

Aphids

Aphids are tiny, soft-bodied sap-sucking insects that look rather like fleas. Those found on ferns may be green or black, occasionally brown or tinged with red; the males have wings. They cluster heavily on new spring growth, feeding off it so that when it unfurls it is distorted. They can be hosed off garden plants; potted plants should be taken outside and hosed and left there for a few days for natural predators like ladybirds and severa (the larvae of the lacewing) to prey on. These predators eat hundreds of aphids each day. Heavy infestations may be sprayed with a soap and water solution (the least toxic to natural predators), or washing soda, quassia chip or nicotine sprays (recipes below). If the pests persist, they can be eliminated with a weak pyrethrum spray. (Pyrethrum is a low-risk, broad-spectrum pesticide which breaks down after a few hours in sunlight without leaving toxic residues. Extracted from the pyrethrum daisy, it kills some beneficial insects, so should be used with care.)

Aphid

Mealy Bugs

Mealy bugs are troublesome pests and are difficult to eradicate. Their bodies are a greyish-white in colour with a texture like cotton-wool or meal, so that when they cluster in the axes of stems and trunks, individual bugs are difficult to distinguish. They are farmed by ants, so it is important to keep ants from reaching infested plants and thus compounding the problem. Light infestations on potted house plants can be removed by touching individual insects with a stick tipped with cotton-wool and soaked in a solution of equal parts of

Mealy bug

water and methylated spirits. Heavier infestations can be hosed off, and the pots left outside where natural predators can consume any survivors. Heavy infestations can be eliminated by spraying with pyrethrum, nicotine, white oil or systemic sprays. Systemic sprays are organophosphate insecticides which enter the sap stream of a plant through the roots or foliage, and are distributed throughout the plant. Modern systemic sprays are less toxic than those which were originally developed during World War II as chemical weapons. However, if you are concerned for your own safety and for the environment, you will use them with care, and only if all other means have not been effective.

White Fly

Greenhouse white flies (*Trialeurodes vaporarium*) are those most likely to attack ferns. They resemble miniature moths and have white wings. Because they cluster underneath fronds they may not be immediately visible. However, if the infested plant is moved, they will swarm upwards in a cloud. Like other sap-sucking insects, white flies secrete honey dew and are farmed by ants for their secretions. Sooty mould may also accompany infestations of white flies. The damage they cause in a small collection of potted house plants will probably be minimal, but they can cause extensive damage to a large collection of ferns with soft fronts. Pots of rhubarb placed amongst such a collection may prove to be an effective deterrent. In the garden, white flies can be effectively controlled with pyrethrum, soap or nicotine sprays.

White fly

Scale

Scale are sap-sucking insects. Their young are mobile; while the mature insects settle in one spot and secrete a waxy protective coating which may be hard or soft. Those with a soft coating

Scale

excrete honey dew and are farmed by ants. Most scale infestations on ferns can be dealt with by spraying with weak solutions of white oil (a low-toxic petroleum oil used to kill the eggs of some insects), but some species of scale are particularly damaging to ferns, so all infestations should be dealt with immediately. Small numbers can be dealt with by crushing the individual insects between the fingers; or wiping the fronds and stipes with a soapy sponge. Natural predators, including ladybirds, the larvae of some species of wasp which lay their eggs in the scale and severa (the larvae of the lacewing), will eat the scale insects on potted plants that are left outside for a few weeks. If infestations are persistent, an environmentally safe insecticide like pyrethrum or nicotine spray can be added to white oil. The scale insects are particularly vulnerable when they are immature and still mobile. Your regional Department of Agriculture should be able to advise you about these times.

Earwigs

Earwigs are elongated, dark brown creatures with pincers on their tails. They collect in leaf litter and debris in the garden, and shade house (greenhouse) and glasshouse corners, and emerge at night to feed. They can damage new growth and should be discouraged. They can be trapped with the aid of rolled, or crumpled, dampened pieces of newspaper, or deterred by a sprinkling of lime around garden plants, and on the floor or benches on which potted plants stand.

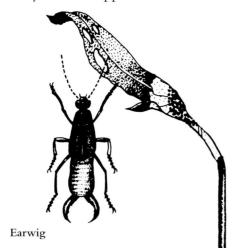

Earwig

Staghorn Beetles

Staghorn beetles (*Halticorcus platyceryi*) are distinctive round beetles about 4 mm (⅛ in) in size, with shiny black wing covers on which are four reddish spots; the larvae are small and pink. They cause damage to the tips and upper surface of the fronds of the *Platycerium* species in the form of pittings like shot holes. In severe infestations, these may merge into large holes and so confuse evidence of the insect. The adult beetles lay their eggs in the new tips so these can be crushed or cut off and burnt. If damage is widespread on large ferns, the adult beetles can be eliminated with a dusting of derris or a pyrethrum spray. Alternatively, one of the home-made sprays like garlic, quassia or rhubarb-leaf (the recipes for which are listed on p. 75) can be used.

Staghorn ferns are also liable to infestations of a caterpillar commonly known as a 'staghorn borer', which is the small grey larva of a small grey moth. It bores into the sterile fronds close to the crown. Repellent sprays may be ineffectual as its shelter is inaccessible, and a poisonous spray like pyrethrum or rhubarb-leaf spray may have to be used to control the problem.

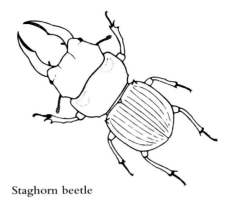

Staghorn beetle

In tropical and subtropical regions, *Platycerium bifurcatum* (elkhorn ferns) are occasionally attacked by the larvae of the elkhorn tip moth. They tunnel into the fertile fronds through the spore patches, causing wilt and browning of the frond tips. Like the staghorn borer, the larvae are inaccessible, and poisonous sprays (such as pyrethrum or rhubarb-leaf) may have to be used to control severe infestations.

Caterpillars

Most caterpillars that feed on ferns are the larvae of moths, not butterflies. They include leaf rollers, loopers, painted apple-moth larvae and fleshy green caterpillars. Damage is usually immediately obvious on the tips of developing crosiers and new fronds. The caterpillars may be the colour of new growth and so difficult to detect. Giveaway signs of the places where they shelter during the day are webbing on the underside of fronds, and fronds bound together similarly. Small infestations can be controlled by removing them with the fingers; or by rubbing off the eggs which are laid in clusters on the underside of pinnae. Sprinkling caterpillars with finely ground black, white or red pepper is also an effective control. Pesticides considered relatively safe, such as derris dust (a botanical insecticide that is of moderate toxicity to predators, but deadly to fish) and the microbial pesticide *Bacillus thuringiensis*, are very helpful in controlling severe infestations. (*B. thuringiensis* is an agent of biological control of pests — it is a bacterial pathogen toxic to caterpillars.) 'Green' gardeners use the roots and leaves of the hellebore plant (Christmas or winter rose) as a substitute for derris.

Looper caterpillar

Cutworms

Moths belonging to the family *Noctuidae* lay their eggs on the host plant. When the eggs hatch, the larvae — called cutworms — migrate to the soil where they cause damage to seedlings by chewing them off at ground level. The prothalli, developing crosiers and fleshy stipes of ferns can also be attacked. Cutworms can be controlled with the same methods as those used for caterpillars. If derris dust is used, it should be lightly scratched into the soil around an affected plant.

Cutworm

Curl grub

Curl Grubs

Curl grubs are the larvae of a group of scarab beetles. They live in the ground feeding on the roots of many plants, including ferns. Affected plants develop a wobble and the soil in the pot will appear constantly wet. An investigation below the surface will reveal a series of tunnels in which the larvae live. Safe herbal sprays like garlic spray do not kill the pest, but they do act as effective deterrents. Curl grubs are best removed from the soil by hand.

Snails and Slugs

Snails and slugs are molluscs and are able to reproduce by self fertilisation. The European snail (*Helix asper*), or common brown snail, can cause a great deal of damage to emerging fronds. If these fronds are continually eaten away, the fern will die. Snails leave a silvery trail of mucus which reveals their presence. Slugs, the most common of which is the fern slug (*Deroceras laeve*), do not leave such telltale signs and are not as easy to detect. In Australia, the native snail is predatory and eats the brown snail. Snails and slugs feed mostly at night and can be caught easily by hand with a torch. Alternatively, they can be trapped using terracotta pots, laid on their sides and filled with lettuce leaves; or with smooth-sided bowls filled with a yeasty liquid like beer or a yeast spread (e.g. Vegemite or Promite) and water. The pests are deterred, and often killed, by substances that scratch and irritate their soft undersides. Slaked lime, alum, crushed egg shells, ground pepper and tobacco dust are some of these substances. Commercial baits usually contain methaldehyde, which breaks down into compounds that are quite harmless to the environment. However,

Common snail

methaldehyde is dangerous to children, birds, cats and dogs, and natural garden predators, and as such, it is advisable that they be avoided.

Recent scientific discoveries may make these baits a thing of the past. Geneticists have discovered how to mass-produce a soil-dwelling nematode less than a millimetre in length which preys on slugs and snails. The molluscs are killed by a bacteria which the nematode conveys to them.

DISEASES

There are few diseases that affect ferns. Those that do are of fungal or bacterial origin. Fungicides and biocides may arrest the diseases, but rarely cure them. Infected plants and soil should be discarded, and pots, tools and staging in shade houses (greenhouses) and glasshouses disinfected. Ferns only succumb to these diseases if conditions are suitable for their growth. Such conditions may be: soil and foliage that is overwet for prolonged periods; or a lack of air flow among crowded plants.

Fungal diseases are recognisable as black and brown spots with fine, hairy growths on them; or as rusty or grey, powdery smudges on leaves and stems. They should not be confused with the fungus 'sooty mould', which lives on the secretions of sap-sucking insects (see p. 66). Infected foliage should be picked off as soon as fungus is obvious, and the plant moved away from others. If fungus persists among a group of potted plants, the humidity should be reduced and any fern that requires high humidity moved away from the group.

TO SPRAY OR NOT TO SPRAY

Most gardeners and fern collectors are in a position to manage the environment in which their plants grow; and to do this in a benign way by encouraging and protecting natural predators and parasites like ladybirds, some wasps, assassin bugs, lacewings and their larvae, spiders, lizards, birds and, under some circumstances, ants. They may use pesticides derived from plants which are poisonous or repugnant to pests, and are often of low toxicity and biodegradable. Traps can be set for some plant predators; and physical deterrents arranged for others. Gardeners have only to be alert, patient, and to persevere, as many herbal sprays are deterrents only, and must be used frequently.

Today, people who are rightfully concerned about the long-term effects of pesticides on themselves and the planet do not have to look far, nor be very resourceful, to find alternatives to damaging and expensive commercial chemicals. Recipes for several environmentally safe garden sprays are listed opposite. Local libraries are an excellent source of information on environmentally sound garden management; local councils and agricultural departments in many countries are now thinking 'green'; and radio and television constantly broadcast programs about ecologically sound methods. There is no need, indeed no justifiable reason, for the home gardener or even the specialised grower to resort to dangerous chemicals which have caused major human health and environment problems in the last few decades, and will continue to unless their use is rationalised.

If dangerous sprays must be used — and some of the recipes listed below are 'dangerous' even though they are naturally occurring poisons and are biodegradable — they should be handled with care. Actual spraying, with its attendant problems of drift, may not be necessary; solutions can be mixed in a bucket and the affected plant dipped or syringed. The manufacturers' instructions on commercial products should be followed carefully — given quantities may be halved and applications repeated at shorter intervals in the case of particularly strong chemicals — and protective clothing should be worn when they are handled. A plant that is in dry soil; is standing in full sunlight; or appears to be ailing should not be sprayed; and spraying on windy days is ill advised. If noxious chemicals must be used, select those that do not linger in the environment and which break down without leaving harmful residues.

RECIPES FOR SPRAYS

Organic sprays, i.e. those which are derived from plants, are of two types: those which are toxic to insects and those which repel them. The most common toxic organic spray, pyrethrum (derived from the pyrethrum daisy), can be bought ready for use in the garden. Home-made rhubarb spray (recipe below) is also a poisonous spray and should be treated with caution. Garlic spray is poisonous to some insects. Home-made nicotine spray (a toxic spray) is less toxic than the commercial preparations.

Organic sprays which repel insect pests can be made at home. They are made from plants which have a strong and, sometimes, repugnant odour, like garlic, onion, marigolds; or like peppers and chillies, which contain an irritating substance. As a general rule, they may be made by mixing equal amounts of the plant and water in a blender, straining off the plant matter and diluting the liquid in the ratio of 1 teaspoonful to 2½ cups of water. These sprays do not remain potent for long, so fresh batches should be made as needed. Home-made sprays which are effective fungicides are: a combination of equal amounts of milk and water; finely ground mustard seeds and water (effective against powdery mildew) (recipe below); garlic spray (which also kills some insects); horseradish spray; washing soda spray (effective against downy mildew) (recipe below); and a spray made from Condy's crystals (recipe below).

Soap and Washing Soda Spray (This spray is used to control sucking insects.)
Add 100 g (3½ oz) shredded soap to 260 g (9 oz) washing soda which has been dissolved in 14 litres (24½ imperial pints, 30 US pints) of water. Heat until the soap has dissolved. Mix together well before spraying.

Condy's Crystals Spray
7 g (¼ oz) potassium permanganate (Condy's crystals); 7 litres (12¼ imperial pints, 15 US pints) water. Combine and spray immediately.

Mustard Seed Spray
Make up in the proportions of 1 part finely ground mustard seeds to 20 parts water.

Rhubarb Spray (poisonous)
1 kg (2 lbs) rhubarb leaves; 3 litres (5¼ imperial pints, 6½ US pints) water. Boil the leaves and water for half an hour, or until the leaves are thoroughly infused.

Combined Onion, Garlic and Chilli Spray (This spray is effective against leaf-eating insects.)
Several of the hottest chillies you can find; 4 large onions; 4 bulbs of garlic; 2 litres of water. Blend, strain and use immediately.

Garlic Spray
Soak 85 g (3 oz) chopped garlic cloves in 2 tablespoons mineral oil (paraffin) overnight. Dissolve 7 g (¼ oz) of an oil-based soap and add the chopped garlic to the resultant liquid. Strain and store in a non-metal container.

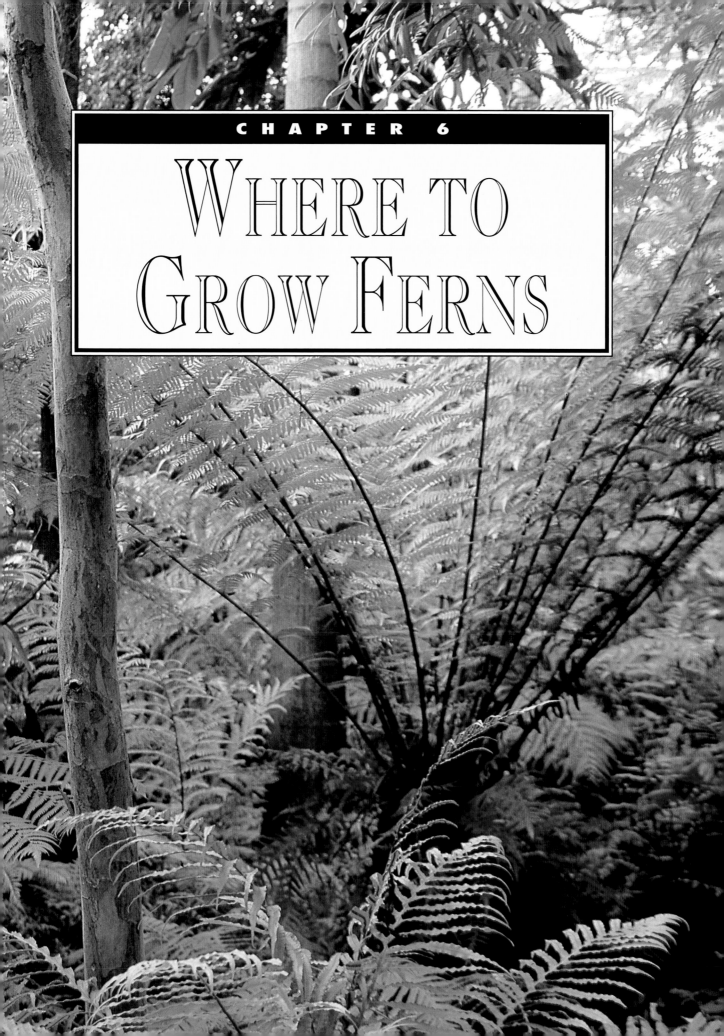

CHAPTER 6

WHERE TO GROW FERNS

Whether grown indoors or in the garden, ferns must be planted with the situation and the prevailing conditions of the particular environment taken into consideration. If these are not ideal, there are a number of steps that can be taken to adapt them to the needs of the ferns.

IN THE GARDEN

Most gardens in the tropical, and in the warm temperate and cool temperate parts of the world have a suitable situation where ferns will grow that is shaded, sheltered and moist. With planning and preparation, and careful selection of the fern species intended for planting, that situation can be an attractive part of the garden. Gardeners in the tropics have a large selection of the luxuriant tender ferns from which to choose; gardeners in warm temperate zones may be able to grow the tender species if the aspect is favourable, but they also have the many hardy species from which to choose; gardeners in cool temperate zones may also choose from the hardy species, and can look forward to the beautiful sight of frost and snow on their fern garden.

Positioning

It is a rather common mistake to believe that ferns should be positioned under trees. In time, the trees will grow upwards and spread, and, if they are evergreen, will cast shade all year round. Their roots will encroach on, and overwhelm the ferns' territory and compete with them for food. They will also act as umbrellas, so that only the most penetrating rain reaches the fronds to wash away dust and grime. When the trees grow high, the ferns will no longer be protected from winds, which may blow away the natural mulch of accumulated leaves, and leave the soil around the ferns bare and eroded. Green flies may infest the trees, dropping their honeydew secretions on the ferns below, so that sooty mould takes hold.

If you are planning a new garden, or a fern bed in an existing garden, place it away from any trees. Ferns grow better in a tree's dappled shade and free from competition for food and water. They grow well among the

Davallia fejeensis

fallen leaves under young deciduous trees, and will continue to thrive there if the shade does not become too dense. If a fern bed under an established tree is desired, pockets of soil among the tree's roots can be dug out without harming the tree. These may be filled with fresh soil which will allow the ferns' roots to establish quickly. Ferns in these pockets will need regular mulching with leaf mould and old cow manure.

ASPECT

If there is no dense shade cast by trees and buildings, a southerly aspect in the Southern Hemisphere, and a northerly aspect in the Northern Hemisphere, should be suitable. These aspects usually do not receive sufficient sunlight to grow flowering plants; however, if they receive sufficient natural or reflected light, and are sufficiently moist and protected, they may suit ferns. A protected easterly aspect that receives only a little morning sunlight should be ideal for many ferns; those growing in an open easterly aspect may need protection during summer from excessive sunlight after the early morning hours. Most western aspects are too hot and the light is too strong for ferns to grow well. If any aspect is completely shaded all day, the choice of ferns will be limited to those that thrive in such conditions.

Adiantum diaphanum

MICROCLIMATE

An understanding of a garden's microclimate is important. The patterns of light and air movement dictated by the position of buildings and trees will create a climate within, and peculiar to, each garden space. With time, this microclimate may alter. It may be changed suddenly by the demolition of a building or the felling of a tree, or the change may occur slowly and naturally as trees grow bigger, cast more shade and alter wind patterns. If you are aware of these changes, and the effects they are having on your plants, you will be able to take steps to counter them.

WIND

Wind is one of a fern's worst enemies. If it is strong, it can distort and batter fronds and retard new growth. After a fern has been established for a while, it will have aligned its fronds to the prevailing winds, so, if natural or man-made protection is lost, and the direction of the wind changes, it may be severely damaged. If some form of protection is needed, a planting of trees or shrubs (or a fence made of laths or lattice, or similar material), which will allow the passage of air, will be more effective against strong winds than a solid wall which will only divert them.

Soil

Good soil preparation is vital. If your soil is not ideal for fern growing, it can be improved, but its fertility will have to be continually monitored to maintain the most desirable conditions.

HEAVY SOIL

If the soil is a heavy loam, it can be made suitable for fern growing with the addition of coarse organic matter, grit and gypsum (see pp. 38–44). These materials will improve aeration and prevent the soil from packing down and becoming hard. Ferns will grow in soil with a heavy texture, but it must be tilled a few months before planting. After planting, leaf mould should be applied regularly as organic matter breaks down and has to

Attractive landscaping with low-growing ferns and selaginella.

be replenished. The soil should be worked prior to planting to a depth of 24–40 cm (10–15 in) for small to medium ferns, and to a depth of about 60 cm (2 ft) for larger species like tree ferns.

SANDY SOIL

This can be made suitable for ferns if plenty of organic matter in the form of peat moss and well-rotted manure is dug in to aid moisture retention. Sandy soil is easily worked and suitable for many ferns, especially the lime-tolerant species and those that grow naturally among rocks. However, because it does not retain water, it will require regular additions of humus. It will also need to be mulched well; and to be watered deeply and frequently.

CLAY

It takes time to get clay into a condition where it is suitable for growing ferns, so it is usually best to dig it out and replace

Sherbrooke Forest, Victoria, Australia.

it with top soil or, alternatively, with introduced soil. Good drainage is necessary to ensure that the clay pan does not form a sump under the fern bed because ferns will not tolerate sodden conditions.

Drainage

Good drainage is essential. After heavy rain, keep a close watch on ground that is intended for a fern bed. If the water remains there for two or more days, the drainage should be attended to before planting. A garden bed may be drained by laying agricultural pipes or perforated plastic drainpipes under, and leading away from, the bed. If drainage is an insurmountable problem, an elevated bed may be the solution; or a rock garden planted with species of ferns that grow naturally with their roots in the cool protection of rocks and stones.

Fertilisers

Immediately before introducing new ferns to a garden bed, a light dressing of bone dust should be dug into the soil. This is a readily available organic food which will give the plants a good start. Chemical fertilisers should not be used at this stage as they may burn tender new roots.

Planning

Plant so that individual ferns can be displayed to advantage and have space for their roots. Large ferns, like the *Polystichum*, *Dryopteris* and some of the *Athyrium* and *Todea* species, need at least 1 m² (1 yd²), and small species need about 30 cm² (1 ft²). Creeping ferns need about 1 m² (1 yd²).

You may be tempted to overplant if you are impatient. However, by doing so, you will lose a great deal of the individual fern's beauty of form and habit. It would be a pity not to be able to admire the perfect rhythm of a *Blechnum*'s unfolding or the shapeliness of a bird's nest fern. It is a pity, too, to see a tree fern jammed into a corner where its graceful branching fronds cannot develop symmetrically; the upward growth of the tree fern is slow, but its fronds spread quickly and need plenty of space in which to spread.

Todea wilkesiana

IN THE SHADE HOUSE (GREENHOUSE)

In a shade house or greenhouse, you can adapt temperature and moisture to the needs of the ferns and grow species that you would otherwise not be able to grow. A shade house (greenhouse) will cut down the amount of sunlight and create shade. It will also affect temperatures, but in cool temperate areas not sufficiently to permit the growing of tropical plants. Ferns that are deciduous when grown outside, may keep their fronds all year round in a shade house (greenhouse). Those that are merely frost-tender in the garden, and those that are semi-dormant, may continue to grow through winter.

A shade house (greenhouse) can be a simple structure and a flexible one. If made of brushwood, laths or shadecloth, the amount of shade required can be regulated by placing the laths or brushwood closer together or further apart; or by selecting a shadecloth that gives the degree of shade required. If shade only is required, just a roof may suffice; if wind is a problem, the sides may have to be screened also. The humidity can be increased readily by keeping the earth floor dampened. In winter, the removal of alternate layers of laths or brush will allow more sunlight to reach the ferns.

Shadecloth is available in a number of densities — 32%, 50%, 70% and 80% being the standard materials. The degree of shade that is required will be dictated by the aspect of the growing area and also by the proximity of overhanging trees, or of nearby buildings (a building that is painted white can be highly reflective). In the Southern Hemisphere, a shade house (greenhouse) with a northwesterly aspect will require a denser shadecloth. The same applies, but in reverse, for a shade house (greenhouse) with a southwesterly aspect situated in the Northern Hemisphere. If a deciduous tree shelters the shade house (greenhouse) during summer, the degree of protection that is required can be greatly reduced.

Acrostichum coenopteris

IN THE GLASSHOUSE

A glasshouse enables you to exercise almost complete control over light, temperature (if it is heated) and humidity, so that many species of ferns can be cultivated. Commercially-made glasshouses and books about growing plants in glasshouses are not intended for fern growers, but instead for the cultivation of hothouse and flowering plants. Glasshouses are usually constructed to attract, and make the most of sunlight; and books about cultivation will advise how to plant and grow the plants that thrive in these conditions. The cultivation of ferns is usually an afterthought when it is found that there is shade underneath the benches provided for the potted plants.

Adapting the Glasshouse for Ferns

Any existing glasshouse, even a glasshouse built in an exposed position, can be made suitable for ferns if the roof and sides are shaded. This can be done by the conventional whitewashing method; the roof should be given a dense coat of whitewash, then a second coat should be applied with a stippled effect, which will create the effect of dappled shade, like that in a fern's natural habitat. Lath blinds make a flexible, long-term, but rather expensive, shading. They can be rolled up during winter to allow more light to penetrate. They should be hung so that the slats run north–south; in this way they will cast shadows quickly as the sun climbs. Blinds can also be made from shadecloth or a light material like scrim. To lengthen

A glasshouse allows the grower almost complete control over light, humidity and temperature (if the glasshouse is heated), so that many species of ferns can be grown.

The old fernery at Ripponlea, in Victoria, Australia, holds an excellent collection of ferns. It is a shade house (greenhouse) constructed with laths, where temperature and moisture can be adapted to grow fern species that would not grow otherwise.

the life of material blinds, hang them inside the roof; but in this position they will not be as effective as blinds hung externally, which will prevent the sun from shining directly on the glass.

An ideal glasshouse for ferns is one that is almost continually lightly shaded. The shaded side of a house can be an ideal location; if a door or window opens directly into it from the house, the world of the fernery will also become a feature of the house. A fernery attached to the house in this way is economical to heat.

Ventilation

Good ventilation is essential to the successful management of a glasshouse so that extremes, and sudden rises and falls of temperature can be avoided. In a commercially-made glasshouse, adequate ventilation will be provided. However, if you build your own glasshouse, ventilation must be planned very carefully, especially if artificial heating is not going to be used. Ventilation is more essential at the top than at the sides, because if the top vents are open, hot air will be able to escape. Openings in the gable ends, or on each side of the roof ridge, or a hood ventilator extending the length of the building, should be adequate.

Temperatures are best managed by admitting air early in the mornings and closing the vents early in the afternoons.

It is necessary to keep air in the glasshouse circulating. During the summertime, damp stagnant air encourages the growth of moulds and bacteria; during winter, it encourages frost. Ventilators should be closed only if a gale, dust storm or fog is threatening; but at least one vent should always be left open on the lee side.

Frost

In an unheated glasshouse, frost may be prevented by lowering the blinds on the roof to conserve heat absorbed during the day; and by providing an effective barrier between the plants and the glass with newspaper or brown paper. It is a good precaution to cut down watering during frosty spells; and to keep the atmosphere as dry as possible, and the air moving. If the ferns do freeze, they should be allowed to thaw gradually — out of direct sunlight. Pots should be lifted off the floor (always the coldest part of a glasshouse) and placed in boxes, or inside larger pots, lined with any material that will insulate the plants' roots against cold and possible freezing.

Heating

A glasshouse, or a growing area that is protected by plastic, can be heated by several means. A small boiler fired by gas, coke, oil or by solar power, and the necessary piping for the hot water circulation, is an old, still efficient method. The pipes maintain a uniform and evenly distributed temperature, and the financial upkeep, after the initial installation costs, is not high. Electrical heating can be arranged by means of a coil system; or by heating the floor, if it is a concrete slab. This type of heating gives an even but dry heat. For fern cultivation, the dryness must be counteracted by humidifiers. Individual kerosene heaters, placed at intervals throughout the house, are the cheapest method of heating. The fumes do not pose a problem if the burners are efficient and the area well ventilated. Large individual gas burners that blow hot air into the house are used by commercial growers; these heaters are suitable for most commercially cultivated plants, but, as the hot draughts can damage foliage, the heaters must be carefully located in a fern-growing house. If the glasshouse is a small one, a convection heater, such as a potbelly stove, may be all that is necessary. In countries where heating costs are not high, low energy infra-red radiant heaters are used by growers, resulting in significant savings on fuel costs. The insignificant running costs of heating with solar energy have to be weighed against the, usually, high costs of installation. However, solar heating technology is continually improving and the cost of installation is coming down; and

Alsophila pycnocarpa

many people are finding it a more suitable alternative to burning fossil fuels, particularly when the costs to the environment are also considered.

As a guide to temperatures in the glasshouse, the following is an internationally accepted scale: cool 7°–15°C (45°–60°F), intermediate 12°–21°C (55°–70°F) and warm 18°–26°C (65°–80°F). The minimum temperature at which tropical ferns are grown should be 12°C (55°F), but many subtropical species will thrive with a minimum temperature of 7°–10°C (45°–50°F). Excessive heat encourages premature growth which is vulnerable to hardship. The most important aspect of heating a glasshouse is that the temperature is kept constant, only varying by a few degrees, and that an even temperature is maintained within a range recommended for a particular fern. If, for reasons of economy, winter temperatures have to be kept lower than those recommended, the fern will not necessarily die, but will probably become dormant and may shed its fronds.

GROWING FERNS INDOORS

A room in one's own house should be an ideal place in which to grow ferns, especially the tender species. The inside air is usually much milder than outside; temperatures are less extreme and less prone to sudden changes; and the light is usually softly filtered through blinds or curtains, even to the point of being gloomy like a fern's natural habitat. Such ideal conditions evidently prevailed in Victorian times and may have been one of the reasons why ferns became such popular house plants.

Humidity

In books about the cultivation of ferns in Victorian times, one reads that the average house always had a kettle boiling on the hearth so that the air was relatively moist. The atmosphere in modern houses with central heating and air conditioning is usually too dry for ferns. This problem should be overcome for ferns to thrive indoors.

GROUPING

Grouping several plants together is an effective way of providing humidity. (All plants give off water vapour through their leaves during the transpiration process and the vapour creates humidity around the plant.) Plants grouped together over a tray or dish that contains water will benefit greatly from the evaporation. Also, they will lose less moisture through the soil surface and the sides of the pot — if the pot is made of porous material — and so will require less watering. It is important that the pots do not stand *in* the water.

SPRAYING

Spraying around ferns with a water-filled atomiser is another effective method of keeping the moisture content of the air high. This is an effective way of increasing the humidity on a particularly dry day. The water in the atomiser should be kept at room temperature and the foliage should not be wetted excessively.

Asplenium nidus

Watering

The correct watering of indoor plants depends on knowledge of the needs of the plants in a particular situation. The soil in a pot that is close to a window will dry out more quickly than the soil in a pot on a table at a distance of a metre (yard) or so from the same window. Several plants grouped together over water will dry out much more slowly than one standing by itself in a dry saucer. The most effective way of watering indoor plants is to take them outside, flood them with a gentle spray from the hose or the watering can, and then let them drain completely before returning them indoors.

CUTTING DOWN EVAPORATION

Evaporation from the soil can be cut down by mulching with peat moss, sphagnum moss, leaf mould, paper or foil; or anything else that will ensure that the soil underneath stays damp. Another effective method is to place the pot in a container that is larger than itself and lined with any of the above materials. This method cuts down evaporation so effectively that the number of times a plant needs to be watered may be halved.

Hazards

WINTER

It is difficult to grow ferns indoors in the winter because of fluctuating temperatures and relatively low light levels. Indoor ferns that thrive during spring and summer, when doors and windows are left open, may be set back in winter when doors and windows are closed and individual rooms are heated at irregular intervals. Ferns growing in centrally heated houses are slightly better off, as temperatures are fairly constant, but they may be set back if the atmosphere is too dry.

The generally lower light levels and fewer daylight hours in winter, which cause some species to become dormant, can be exaggerated indoors. These conditions can particularly cause problems when curtains are closed during winter to retain warmth.

If these conditions prevail, indoor ferns may be better off kept outside for the winter, in a sheltered, frost-free place.

WINDOWS

Temperatures can vary greatly in the vicinity of a window. Glass conducts cold readily, so that the fronds of a fern growing close to a window may be 'burned' by the cold. If the pot, too, is in contact with the glass, the roots may be chilled and damaged. Draughts that enter through ill-fitting joinery are often the likely cause of a fern's not thriving.

FUMES

Fumes from inefficient heating appliances can sometimes be the cause of poor growth. Gas- and oil-burning fires usually have

Arthropteris tenella

sufficient built-in control of their emissions, so that ferns are safe in a house heated this way as long as humidity is maintained and air circulates freely. Ferns are tolerant of mild kerosene fumes, and many glasshouses are heated this way. Direct heat from open fires and heating appliances is more damaging than the negligible fumes they emit if they are well maintained.

Light

A room that has an easterly aspect and that receives morning sunlight is suitable for ferns — if it does not get too hot in summer. A room with a westerly aspect may be too hot and bright. A room facing north in the Southern Hemisphere (south in the Northern Hemisphere) that gets plenty of light, even if only indirect sunlight, for most of the day may be too bright for ferns and they will require protection. A room facing south in the Southern Hemisphere (north in the Northern Hemisphere) that receives plenty of light should be suitable if the ferns get the maximum amount of light entering the room.

If there is one strong direct light source in a room, a fern will tend to grow towards it. If this is not noticed in time, the plant will develop a permanent lean in that direction as its tissues harden; new growth will come from the hardened tissues and will appear as kinks in the fronds. This may be overcome by turning the plant's container frequently.

ALTERING LIGHT LEVELS
Light levels *can* be altered. A sunny room with large windows and walls painted a light colour will be too bright for most ferns. On the other hand, if it is painted a darker colour and the windows are then screened, it may well be ideal. The light level in the same room can also be altered with the raising or lowering of an exterior blind; or with the planting of a deciduous tree that, conveniently, will make seasonal adjustments.

Phlebodium aureum

ARTIFICIAL LIGHT
Ferns can be grown under artificial light. The light should be directly above and close to the plants, and the height of the lamps should be

adjustable to allow for growth. Artificial lights are not uniform in their quality, or quantity, of radiant energy.

Special fluorescent tubes have been developed to simulate sunlight. However, fluorescent (white) lights, which are in everyday use, and which are strong in the blue and violet wavelengths of the spectrum, supply sufficient light for growth and are cooler and less expensive than the specially designed tubes. (The blue and violet wavelengths stimulate phototropism, which is growth towards light; and photosynthesis, which is the manufacture of food.) The radiant energy of the white fluorescent tubes may be increased without scorching plant tissues if a reflector is used. They may also be used successfully in conjunction with less costly, incandescent bulbs. The latter should not be used alone as they are not sufficiently strong in the red and blue wavelengths; and they generate too much heat. (The red wavelengths are known to stimulate photosynthesis; as well as phytochrome, which is the plant material that causes the germination and growth stages.)

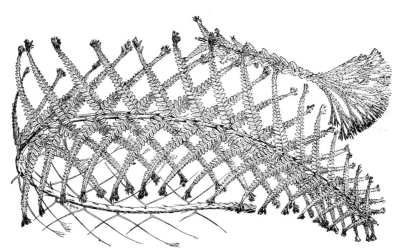

Frond of *Athyrium filix-femina* cv. *Victoriae*.

A cool, or a warm white, artificial light is useful for growing ferns and other shade-tolerant plants. Ferns will require up to 15–20 watts of light per 30 cm² (1 ft²) of growing surface.

All lamps should be changed every one to one and a half years as their radiant energy decreases with time, even though they may still emit light; and, as they attract dust, they should be cleaned regularly to maintain efficiency.

General Maintenance

If conditions are less than ideal, indoor ferns should be placed outside where they will benefit greatly from a few days in the open air, in mild, windless weather, and from showers of rain which will wash house dust from their fronds and accumulated salts from the pot. If indoor conditions are *far* from ideal, it is an advantage to have sufficient plants so that you can alternate them between indoors and outdoors as much as possible.

CHAPTER 7

FERNS IN
CONTAINERS

Ferns thrive in containers. They may stay in the same container for years, needing to be repotted only when their roots are overcrowded and growth becomes thin. If the combination of pot and plant is pleasing, there is no need to reject the original pot. Success depends on a suitable fern, careful potting, an effective drainage system, an appropriate potting mixture and careful watering.

POTS AND POTTING

Suitable Ferns

The smaller ferns will obviously be the best choice for potting. This does not mean that other ferns will not grow in a pot at all. Larger ferns and those that grow quickly, like *Nephrolepis cordifolia* (common fishbone or herringbone fern), *Pteris cretica* (Cretan or ribbon brake), *Adiantum raddianum* (delta maidenhair) and all the tree fern species, will have to be frequently repotted in appropriate containers to maintain steady growth, until eventually they become too large to handle.

Suitable Pots

Any conventional pot or hanging basket made of plastic, earthenware, metal, wood, bamboo or wicker may be used. (Hanging baskets have a section to themselves, see p. 109.) Old iron kettles, china chamber pots or tea pots, if their rustic or interesting character takes the fancy; old laundry troughs of timber or cement; discarded washing machine barrels or coppers; half beer and wine barrels can make interesting containers. Anything that pleases and is an appropriate size and shape may be used if it complements the fern.

Containers should have a large hole in the bottom, or a number of holes around the sides that will let excess water flow away easily. Sometimes the holes in a new terracotta pot will need to be cleared; a masonry drill can be used to improve the holes in a cement tub and a hot poker used on plastic pots.

If you are using pots without drainage holes, care must be taken to provide plenty of drainage material and to ensure that the plant is not overwatered. Ferns do not thrive in a pot without drain holes and should not be kept in them for long.

If ferns are kept outside in plastic pots, the temperature of the soil in the pot will be approximately the same as that of the surrounding air because plastic does not have the insulating qualities of wood or clay. Take this into consideration on a day of extreme temperatures; if the pot is sitting directly on a masonry or metal surface; or if it is close to a surface that reflects heat and cold.

Athyrium filix-femina var. *frizelliae*

CATCHPOTS OR COVERPOTS

These are available in many shapes and sizes and are useful to disguise an ugly pot. They are usually sold with the explanation that they catch the 'drips'. If the drips accumulate in the catchpot and come into contact with the soil in the container pot, they can cause the soil to go sour.

More importantly, catchpots insulate the container and keep the roots at an even temperature. The insulation is made more effective if the space between the two pots is packed with a mulching material like moss or paper.

CEMENT TUBS

These are suited to fern culture; the small amount of lime used in their manufacture does not affect the soil. If left unpainted they remain porous, helping to keep the soil aerated. Their rather raw new look does mellow with time, so that the white and grey pots take on a pleasant weathered look. Large cement tubs should have extra holes bored through the base to make the drainage more effective.

WOODEN TUBS

Large wooden tubs and barrels intended for long-term use should be charred with a blow torch or coated with bitumen to preserve them. They are usually sold with inadequate drain holes so extra holes may have to be bored in their bases.

PANS

Wide shallow terracotta pots, called 'pans' by growers, are ideal for fern growing.

CLAY, WOODEN AND PLASTIC POTS

Clay and wooden pots are closer to a fern's natural growing conditions, but ferns do equally well in plastic or glazed pots if the different qualities of each are understood and kept in mind.

The soil in clay and wooden pots dries out much more quickly than that in plastic or glazed pots, but the former types of pots have the advantage of providing more aeration. The soil mixture used in a plastic pot should be light and should drain readily to compensate for this. Both clay and wood hold moisture so plants will not have to be watered quite as frequently. However, salts and algae are more likely to build up in the porous material.

From left: *Osmunda regalis, Microlepia strigosa, Asplenium bulbiferum.*

Plastic pots, being light and easy to handle, are ideal for the commercial grower as well as for the home gardener, especially one who has an extensive collection of ferns. Plastic pots may not last as long as clay and wooden pots because, depending on the quality of the plastic used, weathering will cause the material to break down. A dropped clay pot, however, is usually a broken pot!

Pots to Avoid

Ferns' roots grow close to the surface of the soil. Any soil beneath the roots may there-fore not always be used and 'sourness' can build up. For

Pots made of clay are close to a fern's natural growing conditions.

this reason, deep pots are not suitable, though they can be adapted with extra crocks. Wooden containers made of treated pine should also be avoided. Although the soft green colour is attractive, it is an indication of the chemicals used in the preservation process. These may seep into the soil and damage roots.

Pots with a neck that is much narrower than the body of the pot are unsuitable for most plants. This is simply because it is almost impossible to remove the plant without damaging both the roots and the pot.

Pots promoted as 'self-watering' should be avoided. A fern in this type of pot cannot be watered thoroughly so that accumulated alkalies are not flushed out of the soil. The soil tends to remain constantly on the wet side of moist and sourness may develop; and a dry side of moist condition, which is necessary at regular intervals to stimulate root growth, is inhibited.

Cleaning Pots

Experienced growers advise: 'Dirty pots carry trouble.' All pots should be cleaned thoroughly before use.

Old pots made of terracotta look attractive with their sides encrusted with mosses and salt, but left in this condition they can be a continual source of fungal diseases. They should be soaked in soapy water, scrubbed and rinsed thoroughly; then scalded with boiling water or rinsed with a disinfectant solution. Plastic pots should be treated similarly. Undiluted vinegar will dissolve any stubborn salt crusts.

Size and Preparation of Pots

The size of the pot depends on the size of the fern that is being planted. The diameter of the pot should be about one-third of the height of the plant. Ferns do not thrive when 'overpotted'. Their roots, which grow slowly and form a dense fibrous mass, should only just fill their container.

Drainage

A good drainage system is essential. Old-fashioned methods, such as a deep layer of broken clay pots (called crocks) placed in the bottom of pots, are now considered unnecessary because modern potting mixtures, many of which are soil-less, are self-draining. This may be so, but many fern growers feel that these mixtures remain too wet for too long and so prefer to rely on a deep layer of crocks or stones to counter this.

To construct an effective draining system in a conventional terracotta pot — i.e. one with one large drain hole in the bottom — the following procedure should be followed. The hole should be covered with a piece of perforated zinc, fine netting or galvanised wire made of plastic, in order to prevent worms, slugs and earwigs from collecting in the pot base.

Sadleria cyatheoides

Utilising the stem of a dead tree fern to accommodate other plants.

A curved piece of broken crock, convex side upwards so that it sheds water and directs it to the hole, is then placed over the hole. This is secured in place with a deep layer of crocks, stones or gravel (the smallest pieces should be used on the top layer). A layer of sphagnum moss, coarse peat or other fibrous material should then be placed on top of the drainage material. (In a large tub, a layer of turf placed with the grassed side down is a good alternative.) This layer of fibre prevents fine soil particles washing down into the crocks and blocking the drain hole.

A 15 cm (6 in) pot, for example, should have about 5 cm (2 in) of drainage material, and a 25 or 30 cm (10 or 12 in) pot about 8 cm (3 in). The tiny 'thumb' pots used for propagation do not need crocking as the plant is not in them for long. A big wooden or cement tub that is being prepared for long-term use should have at least 15 cm (6 in) of crocking and a deep layer of turf, moss or fibre placed over the top of it. If the pot is a particularly deep one, and unsuited to fern roots, the depth of the crocks should be increased accordingly.

Plastic pots that have holes all the way around the sides should be filled with coarse, even-sized stones or gravel to a height just above the holes. Moss or fibre can then be placed on top.

Potting Mixtures

There are many excellent ready-made proprietary brand potting mixtures for ferns. A suitable mixture contains soil, peat moss and sand in approximately equal quantities. If the mixture contains soil substitutes, or synthetic matter, like styrofoam, regular fertilising and careful watering will be necessary as these mixtures become waterlogged readily. If this occurs, increase the drainage material in the bottom of the pot. If the mixture dries out quickly, add more water-retaining material such as peat moss.

Davallia griffithiana

If you wish to make your own potting mixture the following is a good standard for ferns:

> 1 part by volume of good loam, 1 part by volume of coarse sand, and 2 parts of well-rotted leaf mould. To each 4 buckets of this mixture, add a 15 cm (6 in) pot of charcoal pieces, and a 2 cm (1 in) pot of John Innes Base Fertiliser, all thoroughly mixed.

John Innes Base Fertiliser is a fertiliser made up as follows:

> 2 parts by weight of hoof and horn meal 3 mm (⅛ in) grist (13% N), 2 parts by weight of superphosphate of lime (18% P) and 1 part by weight of sulphate of potash (48% K).

Two parts of John Innes No. 1 potting mixture (see below) mixed with one part of sphagnum peat moss is a good mix for ferns. Charcoal pieces should be added to counter any sourness.

The John Innes No. 1 potting mixture is made up as follows:

> 7 parts by bulk of medium loan (that has been sterilised and sifted through a 1 cm (⅜ in) sieve), 3 parts by bulk of horticultural grade peat moss and 2 parts by bulk of coarse sand. To each 4 buckets of this mix add 40 g (1½ oz) hoof and horn meal, 40 g (1½ oz) superphosphate, 20 g (¾ oz) sulphate of potash and 20 g (¾ oz) of chalk.

Both the John Innes base fertiliser and the potting mixture can be bought ready-made. If made at home, it is important not to alter the specified amounts. However, it is possible to follow the formula without sterilising the loam. Soil may be sterilised by steaming or baking in an oven. Be warned, the smell is unpleasant.

Osmunda fibre, which is available in the United States and used as an orchid growing medium, is excellent for ferns. It can be used instead of peat moss in a conventional potting mixture. Sometimes it is available in strips which can be wound around the roots of a small plant and then wedged firmly in a pot.

Planting

Place some potting mixture on top of the drainage material and position the fern on top of this. Spread the roots so that they are not tangled. Add more potting mixture, a handful at a time, and allow it to flow into the spaces between the roots to fill any air pockets. Tap the pot on a hard surface to settle the soil and then gently, but firmly, press it into place. The soil should be 1–2 cm (½–1 in) below the rim of the pot to facilitate watering.

Water thoroughly and gently, and check that the pot is draining well. If the plant wilts, and you are sure that there is plenty of moisture in the soil, spray around the foliage regularly until it revives; a glass cloche or plastic covering will help to prevent further

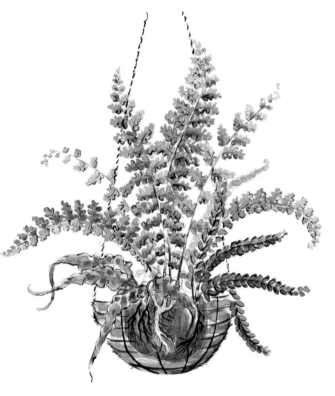

A hanging basket of ferns.

Blechnum occidentale

dehydration. Do not be tempted to give the plant extra water while it is in this condition as the roots will not yet be growing in the new soil and it may turn sour.

OVERPOTTING

Overpotting is one of the causes of failure of potted ferns. The excess soil holds too much moisture in proportion to the active roots; the roots then rot and bacteria in the soil dies, causing a sour odour. A plant will wilt perpetually if its roots are in soil that is wet for too long. If you suspect that the problem is overpotting, examine the soil and the roots. If the soil is slimy and sticky, and the root tips are brown, replant into fresh soil in a smaller pot, after first trimming the roots of any dead matter. It is difficult to revive a plant after a setback like this.

Repotting

Ferns should be repotted when growth is thin in the centre of the plant and when any new growth comes mainly from around its outer edges; or when new growth is yellow and stunted. Ferns prefer to be slightly root-bound, with their stolons and creeping rhizomes pressing against the side of the pot, so they should be put in a new pot that is only one size larger than the original.

Soil should be thoroughly wetted before a plant is taken out of its pot. If it cannot be removed easily, run a sharp knife between the soil and the pot to sever the roots, then turn the pot upside-down and tap it gently on a sturdy, overhanging ledge. Keep your fingers spread over the soil surface to minimise root disturbance. If the roots are compacted and it is difficult to tease away the old potting mixture, the root ball can be rolled gently between your hand and a hard surface. Repot the plant at the original depth, so that roots are not exposed and the foliage is not buried.

INCREASING THE SIZE OF FERNS

A fern can be returned to its original pot and encouraged to grow larger if it is one that can be divided — i.e. a fern that does not form a single crown and has several growing tips. Remove the smallest and weakest portions and any dead parts before replacing it.

DIVIDING

A fern can be divided if it forms a clump with many growing tips. The clump may be cut into four equal segments, and each trimmed of any moribund parts. Each segment should then be placed in a pot that will only just contain it. For example, the four segments from a 15 cm (6 in) pot would each fit comfortably into a 10 cm (4 in) pot. Several of these segments may be planted in a larger container or hanging basket, but their growth is usually slow; better specimens may be obtained by first planting the segments in 8–10 cm (3–4 in) pots to stimulate root growth.

Some of the top growth should be cut back immediately a fern is divided, otherwise the foliage places too heavy a demand on roots that may have been damaged while being repotted.

Routine Care

Old fronds should be cut off close to soil level to allow light and air to reach new growth and to deprive pests like mealy bug and scale of breeding grounds. Maidenhair ferns and other ferns that are dormant or semi-dormant during the winter should have all their fronds cut back or burned off. Burning is effective in controlling pests; the crown of the fern should be rotated over a small fire so that the stubble left by the fronds is charred.

The burrowing activity of earthworms disturbs the roots of small potted plants; they may well be an asset in the garden, but in a pot they are simply a nuisance. Small mounds on the surface of the soil and soil in the saucer under the pot indicate their presence. They can be dug out of the pot with a teaspoon and transferred to the garden, if you are kind-hearted; or they may be destroyed by watering the soil with a weak solution containing diluted insecticide.

Moss and liverworts should not be tolerated growing amongst potted ferns. However, there is an old theory held by growers that moss indicates the health of the fern, so, perhaps, a *little* moss may be tolerated; it has the added advantage that it does look attractive.

Doodia aspera var. *multifida*

AERATING

Potted ferns will benefit if they are lifted a few centimetres or inches off the ground on a rack made of wood or bricks. This permits air to circulate around both pot and plant, and water to flow freely from the drainage holes. The life of a wooden container can be prolonged if it is placed on a rack; a wooden barrel should be rested on its base, not on its staves as these can be dislodged if they have to support too much weight.

MAINTAINING LARGE POTTED FERNS

A large plant growing in a large pot will require regular maintenance to stimulate growth and preserve an attractive appearance. If repotting appears too difficult, each spring, the top soil should be scraped away and replaced with fresh potting mixture containing plenty of bone meal and leaf mould.

Alternatively, a channel, a few centimetres or inches wide, may be cut, as deeply as possible, into the soil around the perimeter of the pot to permit the removal of matted roots and old soil; any accessible roots should then be teased out and the channel refilled with fresh potting mixture that contains bone meal and leaf mould. Both of these methods are effective in stimulating root growth in an old plant; but they are likely to maintain growth and an attractive appearance only, and may not promote *new* top growth.

Ferns that have been in large pots for many years are difficult to water effectively. They tend to wilt readily because, with time, soil and fibrous matter have been compressed or washed away and the roots may be the sole contents of the pot. A hose should be left trickling on the soil and a deep mulch placed on top after watering. Make sure that water comes away from the bottom of the pot as the roots may have blocked the drain hole.

TERRARIUMS
AND BOTTLE GARDENS

The elaborate Wardian cases and fernshades in which the Victorians cultivated their indoor ferns have disappeared along with antimacassars and crinolines. If you wish to pursue the interesting pastime of growing ferns under glass, you may be lucky enough to find a Wardian case in an antique shop, but, more than likely, the only place to see one these days is in a museum, and you will probably have to settle for something more modern in which to cultivate your ferns. Until a few decades ago, nurseries used glass cloches — bell-shaped glasses with a knob on top — to protect their seedlings. These

Once the balance of light and moisture is correct, a terrarium will be self-sufficient. Condensation will appear on the glass to indicate this.

cloches made attractive alternatives to glass shades, but nurseries now use plastic protection and cloches, too, have all but disappeared. However, there are many modern alternatives you should consider: glass carboys; discarded fish aquariums; glass-stoppered sweet and candy jars; any attractive bottles that have held wines and spirits (these have small openings through which it may be difficult to introduce the plants, but this could be overcome by having a glass cutter remove the top section of the bottle at a more accommodating place). You have only to exercise your imagination — and your ingenuity — to create a 20th century version of the Victorians' miniature landscaped fern gardens growing under glass. Once planted and established in a terrarium or bottle, ferns need less care than potted indoor plants require; this may be an encouraging thought for people who are busy, or who are incapacitated, but who wish to enjoy indoor plants.

Choosing the Right Bottle

Practically any bottle may be planted with ferns, but choose those with wide mouths which give easy access for regular trimming or replacement. The atmosphere inside a glassed-in container is ideal for many ferns and they will grow so rapidly that, even within a few months of planting, they may outgrow it.

Preparing the Container

The bottle should be thoroughly cleaned and dried before planting takes place. If the interior is left damp, particles of soil may adhere to the glass walls and spoil the appearance of the little garden. There should be a layer of small stones or gravel on the bottom of the bottle, so that excess water will collect there and not come into contact with the soil. You will be able to see through the glass if too much water is accumulating and be able to adjust the amount of watering accordingly.

Overwatering is the main reason why ferns in a bottle do not grow well; accordingly care must be taken, when preparing the bottle, to avoid this, and to counter it if it does happen. Place a layer of charcoal chips on top of the stones; these will help prevent the soil from going sour. Select a potting mixture that contains more grit than peat moss for good drainage, and sterilise it to destroy weed seeds and nematode worms, both of which will thrive in such conditions and may overwhelm the ferns. Soil may be sterilised by baking in a domestic oven at 93°C (200°F) for 30 minutes.

A terrarium containing an artistically arranged landscape in miniature.

The easiest way to fill a bottle is to use a clear plastic or glass tube with a funnel in the top. The tube can be directed where the soil is needed, and it will be easier to keep the sides of the bottle clean. Adapt the depth of soil to the height of the bottle and the size of the roots. Try to avoid a depth of soil that is too great in proportion to the size of the bottle, because it will spoil the appearance.

Water carefully so that the soil is evenly moist. If the soil if too wet, it may be better to tip it out and start again.

Planting

Choose small plants; a plant with a large root system may be damaged if it has to be forced through a small opening. Some growers sell plants in tubes which are ideal for this purpose (a tube is a seedling pot about 30 mm (1¼ in) in diameter). They may be difficult to obtain because most commercial growers do not market them at such an early stage in their development; it is unprofitable and such small plants are not hardy. If you are able to secure them, plant them as soon as possible so that they do not suffer a setback. Check all the plants you use for pests and diseases before putting them in a bottle garden; insects and fungi will thrive in the moist atmosphere.

Planting and maintaining a fern garden in a bottle requires dexterity, ingenuity and patience. You will have to improvise, making use of sticks, wire and lengths of cotton to lower and manoeuvre the plants into place; as well as an assortment of contrived devices to tamp down the soil, to water and, later, to do any necessary pruning.

It may take a number of days to establish the balanced conditions that are needed for the garden to become self-sufficient. When the balance has

Pteris cretica var. *albo-lineata* growing in an urn.

been achieved, droplets of water will appear on the inner sides of the container and trickle down to the soil where they will be absorbed by the roots and transpired through the leaves to condense again on the glass. Water should be added gradually to achieve this balance. The container may or may not be stoppered.

Maintenance

A terrarium should be kept in a situation where there is plenty of light, but avoid direct sunlight, which, when intensified by the glass, will be harmful. If the glass is coloured, or thick, extra light may have to be provided. If any flowering plants have been planted together with the ferns, their dead flowers should be removed promptly because they will harbour fungus growth.

Careful observation of the surface of the soil may be rewarding. There, in such ideal growing conditions, you may see the beginnings of new fern growth — the prothalli and young sporophytes.

Suitable Plants

For a very small bottle or terrarium, say about 15 cm (6 in) in diameter, it is probably best to use the *Selaginella* species (club mosses) and the mosses. Some of the smaller species of this genus are:

- *Selaginella brisbanensis*
- *S. gracillima*
- *S. australiensis* and
- *S. apus.*

For larger containers, suitable ferns to grow are:

- *Adiantum capillus-veneris* (southern maidenhair), *A. hispidulum* (rough maidenhair), *A. raddianum* (delta maidenhair), *A. aethiopicum* (common maidenhair) would be suitable in a very large terrarium. The cultivars cv. Gracillimum, cv. Pacific Maid and cv. Pacotti are also suitable.
- *Anogramma* — any of this genus of tiny short-lived ferns.
- *Asplenium flabellifolium* (necklace fern) and many others of the spleenwort species, *A. trichomanes* (common or maiden spleenwort) in particular.
- *Blechnum penna-marina* (alpine water fern).
- *Cystopteris fragilis* and *C. filix-fragilis* (brittle bladder ferns).
- *Doodia* (rasp or hacksaw ferns) — many of this genus are dwarf growing. *Doodia caudata* (small rasp fern) is particularly suitable.
- *Hymenophyllum* (filmy ferns). These ferns enjoy the high humidity in an enclosed bottle.
- *Nephrolepis exaltata* var. *bostoniensis* (Boston fern). The dwarf cultivars cv. Childsii and cv. Miniruffles are also suited to bottle growing.
- *Polypodium vacciniifolium* alt. *microgramma vaccinifolia*.
- *Pteris* (brake ferns) — the smaller cultivars, *P. cretica* cv. Wilsonii and *P. cretica* var. *Albo-lineata* are suited to growing in a bottle.

FERNS IN HANGING BASKETS

While many ferns grow well in hanging baskets, they are particularly suited to epiphytes because the light airy conditions are close to those in their natural habitat.

Galvanised wire baskets; terracotta containers with holes near their rim through which chains or ropes may be passed; pots made from the trunks of tree ferns and from redwood (both of which will not rot readily), which are screwed, not nailed, together and suspended by firmly attached galvanised chain or wire; good quality plastic pots with a saucer attached — these are all suitable for ferns. Well-designed and sturdy containers

Hanging basket containing *Platycerium hilii* and *Asplenium polyodon*.

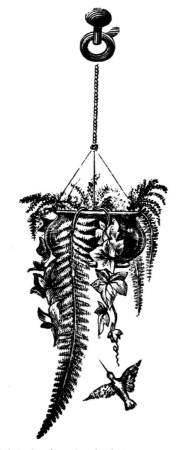

A Victorian hanging basket.

will not disappoint by falling apart after only a few waterings, hanging off-centre or proving impossible to replant.

Wire baskets made of heavy gauge galvanised wire that will not buckle, and that are supported adequately, are the most versatile containers; and ideal for epiphytes. (Plastic pots are suitable to terrestrial ferns.) They are simple and relatively inexpensive to prepare and hang, but their success does depend largely on the material used as lining. It should be attractive as well as durable because, until plants are well established, a large portion of the container will be on view.

Sphagnum moss, paperbark, and osmunda and coconut fibre, all of which are visually pleasing, natural and readily available from nurseries, make ideal linings. However, they should all be used in generous proportions because they break down with watering and weathering. (In many countries it is illegal to take these materials from their natural habitat; if you buy them from a dealer, be sure that you are not supporting someone who is a vandal.)

When using sphagnum moss, line the container to a depth of at least 8 cm (3 in). If this moss is kept moist, it may continue to grow and add to the attractive appearance of the basket. Paperbark is easier to handle if it has been softened before use by soaking in warm water. Holes may be made in the sides of a basket that is lined with any of the above materials, and small hanging ferns and species of *Selaginella* (club mosses) may be planted in the holes. These plants may have to be secured by some means, until roots have taken hold. The creeping rhizomes of ferns, like the *Nephrolepis* genus (fishbone ferns), will quickly find any weak sections in a lining made of natural fibres, and push their way through, adding to the attractive appearance of the hanging basket. The above linings may be used in combination; a basket lined with paperbark and edged with sphagnum moss looks particularly attractive; one lined with paperbark on top and sphagnum moss on the base will drain readily.

Paperbark, moss and fibre linings are expensive when used in large quantities. A compromise may be made by using a lining of opaque plastic, then disguising it with a thin layer of one of the more attractive linings. Carpet underfelt, canvas and hessian are cheaper and effective alternatives. However, since these materials decay readily, it is necessary to provide a deep layer.

If the wire basket is a large one, and it does not matter if the lining takes up a large portion of the interior, pieces of the bark shed by trees, or the fibrous sheaths that form on the trunks of palm trees may be used. They make excellent, long-term linings but may have to be lined themselves with a layer of fine plastic mesh to contain the soil.

Hanging baskets dehydrate quickly. As a precaution against this, any of the listed materials may be lined with a layer of opaque plastic. (Clear plastic is not suitable as it will allow light to penetrate to the roots.) Plastic will also help insulate the container, but holes should be made in the base so that the soil will drain.

Hanging baskets made of terracotta or glazed ceramic material are ideal for terrestrial ferns, but large containers may prove too heavy to handle. These containers are often fitted with rope or twine supports which, if they are in contact with the soil, will rot through quickly. The unglazed, shallow terracotta pots with holes moulded in the sides — the type of pot used for orchid culture — are ideal for epiphytes. However, the holes are usually large and the material itself porous, so a mulch should be used and careful attention paid to watering as ferns require more water than orchids.

Most small-growing ferns are suitable for hanging baskets. Epiphytes are ideal as they will thrive in light, airy conditions; on the other hand, the fronds of terrestrial ferns may be damaged through a lack of humidity, especially if they are growing indoors. Ferns with pendulous fronds, and those that creep, are shown to great advantage in a hanging basket.

Ferns can be planted in combination with other plants.

Ferns may be planted in pleasing combinations with other plants, but they will require extra care if planted with dominant species, such as ivy, members of the *Asparagus* genus and the variegated or ribbon plant. Flowering plants planted among ferns in hanging baskets look attractive, but few plants that continue to bloom in the shaded situations required for ferns. On the other hand, orchids may grow well with epiphytes.

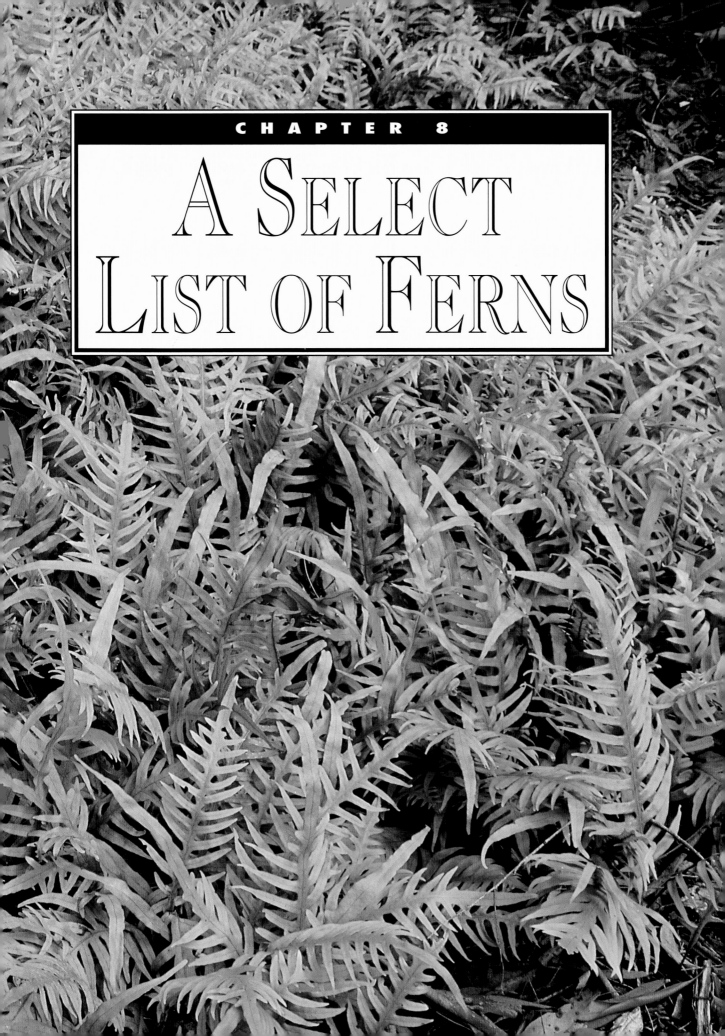

CHAPTER 8

A SELECT LIST OF FERNS

The following list contains almost 200 species of the estimated 10 000 fern species in the world. They are, with few exceptions, ferns that anyone can grow in a house, in a garden, in a glasshouse, shade house or greenhouse, or on a protected balcony or windowsill. Some may have special requirements such as a certain degree of heat in the winter; if so, this is stated in the text. With few exceptions, they are ferns that are readily available in commercial nurseries, through specialised growers or through the buyng and selling of spores and plants among fern society members.

Only a few of the ferns listed are rare or rarely grown, and for these, botanical descriptions and any known cultivation notes have been included because they are mentioned in earlier chapters as being historically or botanically interesting; or have been used as food, medicines or other saleable commodities. Ferns that are well known because of their attractive form have been included even if they require growing conditions that the average gardener may not be able to meet. This has been done so that the list is as comprehensive as possible and may be used as a reference for popular ferns throughout the world.

The main list contains terrestrial, epiphytic and lithophytic ferns. Tree ferns, aquatic ferns, filmy ferns and the fern allies and masqueraders are listed separately. Confusing botanical names and synonyms are cross-referenced. Common names are included after the scientific name with the name of the country where they are used.

The lists are arranged alphabetically by the scientific name, i.e. genus and species; followed by cultivars, varieties, subspecies or forms. The use of this

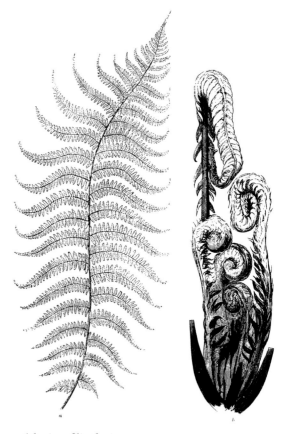

Athyrium filix-femina

terminology is universal and determined by standards set by the International Rules of Nomenclature, which give each plant one name, and one name only. From time to time, the discovery of new facts about a particular plant's structure or reproductive method has led to changes in its scientific name, and it has been moved from genus to genus according to the latest botanical theory. In such a case, it has been noted in the text and cross-referenced, thus lessening the confusion and bringing the reader up to date with the latest terminology.

Individual species may vary. The variations may be to do with the spore-bearing parts or frond structure, which are due to hereditary or environmental factors; or which have been cultivated by growers. These differences within a species are labelled 'cultivar', 'forma' and 'varietas'. A cultivar (cv.) is a plant that has been 'improved' under cultivation. A forma is so called when the changes have occurred in the natural environment and have remained constant through several generations. *Athyrium filix-femina*, the lady fern, because of its genetic instability, is an example of a species that has given rise to hundreds of formae in its natural habitat. When changes have occurred naturally in the same species growing in different geographical areas, the species are classed as varietas (var.). Subspecies (subsp.) is a term used in the same way as varietas. Any changes in species are only noted by botanists if they are stable and have occurred in several generations.

Terms Used in Botanical and Cultural Notes

A small-growing fern is one that is less than 30 cm (1 ft) high, a medium fern is one that is between 30 and 90 cm (1 and 3 ft) high and a large one grows to over 1 m (3 ft). A large plant usually has the equivalent amount of spread and this should be taken into consideration when planning and planting.

A deciduous fern is one that drops all its leaves, even in warm temperate climates. An evergreen fern is one that retains its leaves throughout the winter, even if conditions are freezing.

Ferns in the list are referred to as 'hardy', 'semi-tender' and 'tender'. A hardy plant is one that will withstand long periods of freezing temperatures — they are plants from the cool temperate parts of the world. Semi-tender ferns are from subtropical areas and will not stand frost or temperatures below 15°C (60°F) at night. Tender ferns need either indoor or glasshouse protection, and extra warmth in cool temperate areas, so that temperatures in the growing area does not fall below 15°C (60°F) at night and 18°C (65°F) during the day.

Adiantum formosum

TERRESTRIAL, EPIPHYTIC AND LITHOPHYTIC FERNS

ADIANTUM

Maidenhair Ferns

A genus of mostly terrestrial and small- to medium-growing ferns. The common characteristic of all but a few of the 200 or so species is the separate leaf stalk on all the pinnae or leaflets. It is these remarkably fine filaments that give the fronds the 'floating on air' look. Even the comparatively heavy leaflets of the varieties like *Adiantum peruvianum* are supported on these strong but delicate, dark filaments. The filaments give the genus its common name, 'maidenhair'.

Unfortunately, they are not the easiest ferns to cultivate for they must have high humidity in the air around them. They are hardy in many respects, but can be quickly destroyed if placed in the dry atmosphere of an average house.

Members of the *Adiantum* genus are strong-growing plants that thrive in the garden, or in a pot where their roots are confined, but because of that confined space they need regular feeding to maintain luxuriant growth. The soil for a potted maidenhair should be kept on the dry side of moist so that it is well aerated and the roots are constantly stimulated to seek water. The potting mixture should be gritty with coarse fibre mixed through it to assist the drainage and aeration. Most species do well in soil that contains some limestone component such as marble chips, bone meal, agricultural lime and oyster shell. (At the New York Botanical Gardens, maidenhair ferns are fed a twice-yearly application of a lime in water suspension — one to two teaspoons to a bucket of water — and grow so well that they have to be divided twice a year.)

In temperate areas growth in many species slows down in autumn (fall) and by winter the fronds have died back. Old growth should be left in place where the climate is cold to protect the main body of the plant, and cut off just before spring growth appears; if left on the plant after the spring growing stage, it excludes light and air, and may sometimes distort new fronds. Watering must be cut down during the dormant period to prevent the rhizomes from rotting.

The centre of a plant that has been in a pot for a few years may die if the feeding has not been regular, and if the roots and old fronds have become matted. New growth can be stimulated by repotting; or by cutting out the dead centre portion, and filling the hole with a potting mixture rich in leaf mould. If a plant shrivels because the soil has dried out or the atmosphere has been too dry, it may be possible too revive the fern by cutting off the dead fronds and watering thoroughly. However, it may take some time before the plant looks attractive again.

Adiantum capillus-veneris

Adiantum formosum

Adiantum hispidulum

ADIANTUM AETHIOPICUM (common maidenhair). One of the best known and widespread Australian native ferns with a slender reddish-brown stipe. The pinnules are delicate and wedge shaped. Very easy to grow and quite vigorous, it will quickly outgrow a pot. It grows best in a semi-protected position in the ground in an area that is not totally shaded.

ADIANTUM CAPILLUS-VENERIS (southern maidenhair, Venus's hair). Known commercially as *A. chilense* in the United States, this is a species that is widespread throughout the world, though it is now rare in Great Britain, and can only be found in coastal areas in the southwest. In Australia, it is found in tropical areas growing in rock crevices close to water, but it is not common. It makes a fairly hardy house plant, tolerating low light conditions if the atmosphere is not too dry and the soil is always kept moist.

ADIANTUM CAPILLUS-VENERIS CV. IMBRICATUM (green petticoats). A popular cultivar that is difficult to grow. It likes a low to medium intensity light, a basic soil condition or potting mix, and to be kept moist.

ADIANTUM DIAPHANUM (filmy maidenhair). Native to Australia, New Zealand, Asia and Polynesia, this is a delicate-looking, but easily grown, fern. It has small, usually unforked fronds, and distinguishing black hairs on the pinnules. It tolerates low to medium intensity light and does well in pots, if kept moist. Extensive patches grow in sheltered situations.

ADIANTUM FORMOSUM (giant maidenhair, Australian maidenhair or black stem maidenhair). Found in Queensland, New South Wales, Victoria and New Zealand, this large-growing and vigorous species is easily grown and suits open garden situations, or a large pot.

ADIANTUM HISPIDULUM (rough maidenhair, rosy maidenhair or five-finger Jack). Native to Australia, New Zealand, Asia and Africa, this fern is easy to grow. It is well suited to a rock garden or hanging basket. The new fronds are a delicate pinkish bronze.

ADIANTUM PEDATUM (American maidenhair, five-finger fern). Dainty and distinctive, native to North America, this is a small-growing, hardy species with palm-like, pea-green pinnules. Tolerates deep shade.

ADIANTUM PERUVIANUM (silver dollar). One of the largest, most beautiful species, with broad oval-triangular blades which mature in shades of pink to metallic green. The fronds may reach 1 m (3 ft) long. It is tender and must have warm, moist conditions.

ADIANTUM RADDIANUM (delta maidenhair — also known as *A. cuneatum* and *A. decorum*). A semi-tender, rapidly growing small- to medium-sized plant with filmy pea-green fronds. Native to Central America, it requires high humidity, particularly if grown indoors. It is tolerant of shade.

Adiantum peruvianum

ADIANTUM RADDIANUM CV. FRITZ LUTH. This fern is readily available and is characterised by its steel blue, shingled pinnules. It is an excellent house plant if kept moist, but is semi-tender and requires protection if grown outside.

ADIANTUM RADDIANUM CV. MICROPINNULUM (baby's tears). Like many other plants with tiny leaflets, it looks quite diaphanous and shimmering and, because of this, is very popular. Unfortunately, it is difficult to grow; it is semi-tender and requires high humidity.

ADIANTUM RADDIANUM CV. PACIFIC MAID. A compact, small-growing plant with a strong contrast in colour between new and old growth; the new pinnules are a bright yellow-green. It makes a good house plant, being tolerant of low to medium light conditions.

ADIANTUM RADDIANUM CV. VARIEGATUM. As its name suggests, this cultivar is variegated, the frond tips having a number of white stripes. The wide fronds vary from upright to pendent and so it makes an attractive basket plant; though a large basket will be necessary.

Adiantum pedatum

Adiantum reniforme

Adiantum trapeziforme

ADIANTUM RENIFORME. Originally from the Canary Islands, where it flourishes in limestone crevices, this is a small-growing unusual plant with large, kidney-shaped pinnules on delicate but deceptively strong-looking stalks. It is difficult to cultivate, needing a growing environment of warmth and high humidity.

ADIANTUM TENERUM (brittle maidenhair). This is a small- to medium-growing, tender species that is native to the American tropics. Under cultivation, it is tolerant of low light conditions and must be kept moist.

ADIANTUM TENERUM CV. FARLEYENSE. A cultivar that has been much admired since its discovery in Barbados in 1865, when it was called 'queen of the maidenhairs'. A combination of rosy-coloured new growth and light green old growth makes this a very attractive plant. Like the species, it is tender and rather difficult to grow, needing glasshouse conditions.

ADIANTUM TENERUM CV. WRIGHTII. A plant named by the trade in the United States, but not registered. It is a choice house plant and looks attractive on an elevated pedestal or in a hanging basket as the fronds droop considerably.

ADIANTUM TRAPEZIFORME (diamond maidenhair). One of the biggest species of the genus, this is an unusual maidenhair with large, diamond-shaped pinnules borne on arching fronds. It is tender and requires glasshouse or greenhouse conditions and extra humidity if grown indoors, to duplicate the tropical conditions of its original habitat in tropical America.

ADIANTUM VENUSTUM. This is a hardy species which, more than likely, came from Canada. The bluish appearance of the mature fronds is a particular feature of this small-growing plant. It grows well in a rock garden.

AGLAOMORPHA

A genus of about ten species of large, coarse epiphytes which form spreading crowns of foliage. In their native areas of Sumatra, New Guinea, Malaysia and India, they grow on trees and rocks. They are not commonly cultivated.

AGLAOMORPHA GOERINGIANUM PICTUM (Japanese painted fern — also *A. niponium* cv. Pictum). This is a colourful, hardy fern. The long 60 cm (24 in) fronds are an attractive combination of wine red with a central band of grey-green merging to green at the margin. Easy to grow and very hardy.

AGLAOMORPHA HERACLEA (also known as *Polypodium heracleum*). A tender species that needs plenty of light, high humidity, slightly moist soil and good drainage, as well as protection from direct sunlight and frost. The base of each frond has the shield-like look of the *Platycerium* genus. This species is suitable for a large pot or basket.

Aglaomorpha heraclea

AGLAOMORPHA PYCNOCARPON (glade fern, narrow-leaved spleenwort). A slender, graceful fern from the North American woodlands. The fronds grow in almost circular clusters. It is deciduous and considered very hardy in the ground or in a pot.

AGLAOMORPHA THELYPTEROIDES (silver glade fern or silvery spleenwort). This is a distinctive, strong-growing and hardy fern from North America. The silvery indusia give this fern its common name. It is further distinguished by the underside of the fronds which are covered in pale yellow hairs.

ANGIOPTERIS

Primitive Ferns

This is a genus of about 100 very primitive ferns, some fossil remains of which have been found in rocks of the late Palaeozoic era. They are massive, easily grown plants, and make a wonderful garden feature if they are given plenty of room to develop.

ANGIOPTERIS EVECTA (king fern or giant fern). A giant and primitive member of the fern family that is native to Malaysia and the northern parts of Australia's east coast. The fronds are reputed to be the largest in the fern world and have a strange, fleshy, unfern-like look. The plant is hardy and easy to grow, but must have plenty of room to be shown to full advantage.

ANOGRAMMA

A genus of only a few species of small, smooth, delicate ferns that are widely distributed in temperate regions.

ANOGRAMMA CHAEROPHYLLA. This is a small, dainty fern which may consist of only a few light green fragile fronds. It is native to the temperate and subtropical regions of Central and South America, Europe, Africa, Australia and New Zealand.

ANOGRAMMA LEPTOPHYLLA (annual fern). A tiny fern similar in form and habit to *A. chaerophylla*. It also is suitable for terrarium culture, but care should be taken to water sparingly after the fronds die back.

ARACHNIODES

A genus of 50 or so medium-sized terrestrial species which are found in Southeast Asia, Japan, the Americas and Africa. The fronds, divided into three or four pinnae, are shiny with a harsh feel and have sharply pointed pinnules.

Arachniodes aristata variegatum

ARACHNIODES ARISTATA (prickly shield fern). This species is found in Southeast Asia, Polynesia and as far south as Australia. It is an easily cultivated, if somewhat slow-growing, fern. It is a handsome plant but has a harsh and prickly feel. This fern colonises stream and creek edges by means of its long, creeping rhizome. If cultivated in the garden, it should be provided with some protection from sun and wind.

ARACHNIODES ARISTATA VARIEGATUM. A hardy fern from Japan which is commonly cultivated in Great Britain. It has a yellowish variegation running up the centre of each frond.

ASPLENIUM

Spleenworts

A mixed genus containing species as simple and as stylised as a bird's nest fern and as complicated as a mother fern. The genus is large, consisting of some 650 or so species distributed throughout the world, and containing both epiphytic and terrestrial ferns. There are many hardy species for cultivation.

Asplenium species or spleenworts make excellent potted plants and are hardy inside the house if the humidity is fairly high and constant.

Asplenium bulbiferum

A well-balanced potting mixture is suitable for container growing, even for the epiphyte species. The epiphytes grow well in hanging baskets.

The spleenworts that carry bulbils can be propagated easily from plantlets. (See 'Propagating and hybridising', pp. 58–59.)

ASPLENIUM ADIANTUM-NIGRUM (black spleenwort). Found throughout Europe, Asia, Africa, Hawaii and North America. The common name comes from the colour of the stems below the rachis. It is a small-growing, hardy plant needing medium light and moist conditions with good drainage.

ASPLENIUM ATTENUATUM. An easily grown, hardy, but variable Australian species with long, graceful pointed fronds which form masses of plantlets on the tips. Although very slow growing, it is hardy and makes a good pot plant.

ASPLENIUM BILLOTTII. See *A. lanceolatum*.

ASPLENIUM BULBIFERUM (mother fern, hen and chickens fern, mother spleenwort). Found in eastern Australia, New Zealand and Asia, this is a common and easily grown house or garden plant which is tolerant of shade. The fronds grow to about 1 m (3 ft) in length and are covered continuously with miniature reproductions of the parent plant. They droop gracefully under the accumulated weight of plantlets and so make an excellent basket or pot plant. A mature plant needs a garden position.

ASPLENIUM CETERACH. See *Ceterach officinarum*.

ASPLENIUM DAUCIFOLIUM (Mauritius spleenwort — also known as *A. viviparum*). A small-growing fern similar to *A. bulbiferum*, but in this case the plantlets have teardrop-shaped leaflets with fine scalloping around the edges, giving the plant an unusual grace. It is considered an easily grown plant for indoors, the glasshouse or fern garden.

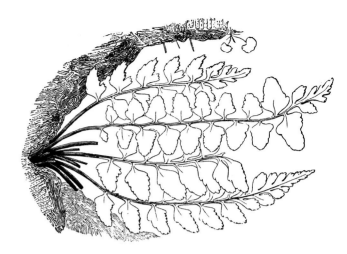

Asplenium marinum

ASPLENIUM FALCATUM (sickle spleenwort). Found originally in Australia, New Zealand, Papua New Guinea and Asia, this fern is now widely grown throughout the world. In its natural habitat it usually grows as an epiphyte on fallen tree fern trunks and in the pads of established staghorn and elkhorn ferns. Because of its epiphytic habit and long fronds that are mostly pendulous, it grows well and looks attractive in a hanging basket.

ASPLENIUM FLABELLIFOLIUM (necklace fern). From Australia and New Zealand. This species has long, narrow fronds and widely separated pinnae, giving it the distinctive appearance from which it gets its common name. This fern colonises rocky places where it grows naturally by forming new plants at the tips of the fronds. It is a weak, but easily grown plant suitable for a pot, hanging basket or sheltered position in the garden.

ASPLENIUM FLACCIDUM (hanging spleenwort, weeping spleenwort — also known as *A. mayi* and *A. majus* in the trade in the United States). From Australia, New Zealand and some Pacific islands, this is a variable species. Most of the ferns of this species have narrow, pendulous fronds, often finely dissected, which gives them a dainty appearance.

It is easily grown in a pot and also looks attractive in a hanging basket.

ASPLENIUM FONTANUM (smooth rock spleenwort). A dwarf, hardy, tufted fern from the southern and central mountain areas of Europe. The narrow fronds are dark green on top and pale green underneath. It grows well in a rock garden or in a small pot with a gritty potting mixture.

ASPLENIUM LANCEOLATUM (lanceolate spleenwort — also known as *A. billottii*). This is a dwarf fern that is ideal for growing in rock gardens in coastal districts. It grows naturally in crevices on cliff faces along the Atlantic Ocean. It is similar in appearance to, and is therefore often confused with, *A. adiantum-nigrum*. However, the fronds of the lanceolate spleenwort are narrower towards the base than those of the black spleenwort.

ASPLENIUM MARINUM (sea spleenwort). A British variety of spleenwort which is tolerant of sea spray. It has glossy green fronds and purplish-brown stems, making it a handsome potted plant. If grown indoors it needs humidity. An Australian spleenwort tolerant of seaside conditions is *A. obtusatum*.

ASPLENIUM MAJUS. See *A. flaccidum*.

ASPLENIUM MAYI. See *A. flaccidum*.

ASPLENIUM NIDUS (bird's nest, crow's nest fern). The bird's nest fern is one of the most widely grown epiphytes. Many people are surprised to find that it is an epiphyte, because it is usually seen growing in the ground or in a pot. It is one of the rare ferns whose leaves are entire — most ferns' leaves are cut or dissected into leaflets. It makes an ideal potted plant because the root system is small in relation to the rest of the plant. When grown in a pot, the soil should be gritty and porous; if grown in the ground, there should be plenty of humus in the soil so that it

is easy for its rather delicate root system to penetrate. This fern grows best in situations of light shade and broken sunlight.

The bird's nest fern can be propagated from spores, or, if it has outgrown its pot or situation, it can be divided. This is best done in the spring. The plant should be cut into four equal portions and the foliage of each portion should be cut back to about 15 cm (6 in) from the crown before each segment is replanted. Eventually, with reasonable care, each new plant will become symmetrical, but this may take a year or two.

ASPLENIUM POLYPODIUM. See *A. falcatum*.

ASPLENIUM RHIZOPHYLLUM. See *Camptosorus rhizophyllus*.

ASPLENIUM RUTA-MURARIA (wall rue spleenwort). A small plant that is common throughout Britain where it is found on rocks and old mortared walls. It can be grown in pots, if the drainage is good, and is considered hardy in most conditions, though this fern is slow to establish.

ASPLENIUM SCOLOPENDRIUM (hart's-tongue fern — also known as *Scolopendrium vulgare*, *Phyllitis scolopendrium*). This fern has many cultivars including 'Crispum' (deeply frilled like a ruff), 'Cristatum' (fronds terminate in crests or tassels), 'Fimbriata' (deeply and finely fringed, frilled margins), 'Marginatum' (narrow fronds, closely lobed), 'Muricatum' (frilled fronds covered with rough projections all over the surfaces), 'Ramo-cristatum' (narrow, many-times branched fronds terminating in flat crests), 'Undulatum' (frond margins gently undulate) and 'Variegatum'. All are hardy and commonly cultivated plants. They are well known to most gardeners because of their strap-like, leathery fronds. These are usually glossy — some with wavy, some with deeply ruffled edges — all with precisely linear sori. The plant is extremely

Asplenium nidus

Athyrium filix-femina

tolerant of most conditions, including frost, but susceptible to overwatering. It can be propagated by inserting basal pieces of the stipe in a propagating mixture.

ASPLENIUM TRICHOMANES (common spleenwort, maidenhair spleenwort). Common throughout Britain, this is a low-growing, spreading plant with long slender fronds and pinnules of maidenhair fern form, which are regularly spaced along the frond. It is hardy and grows well in a rock garden, where it will tolerate some sunlight and dry periods. Limestone should be added to its soil in the garden or in a pot.

ASPLENIUM VIVIPARUM. See *A. daucifolium*.

ATHYRIUM

Lady Ferns

A genus of medium- to large-growing ferns which are widely distributed throughout the world. It has many forms, most with delicate and finely divided fronds that give them a soft, attractive appearance. There are many forms suitable for cultivation. The common name is misleading — it comes from the fern's soft appearance.

ATHYRIUM AUSTRALE (austral lady fern). A well established plant of this species will, under ideal conditions, develop a hardy and woody trunk and elongated fronds so that it looks like a tree fern. A species native to subtropic and temperate regions of eastern Australia and New Zealand, it is easily grown if it is given plenty of moisture and protection from the wind.

ATHYRIUM FILIX-FEMINA. Together with its varieties and cultivars, this is probably the most common of all ferns found in the temperate regions of the Northern Hemisphere. The many beautiful varieties

Athyrium australe

are widely and easily cultivated and grow rapidly. They have even been paid literary tributes, among them Gellatley's 'Song to the Deerhounds' in Sir Walter Scott's novel *Waverley* (1814):

> *Where the copse wood is the greenest,*
> *Where the fountain glistens sheenest,*
> *Where the morning dew lies longest,*
> *There the Lady Fern grows strongest.*

ATHYRIUM FILIX-FEMINA CV. CORYMBIFERUM. A heavily crested cultivar, the crests dividing in several places to give a bundled tasselled effect. It is small, hardy and easily grown, and one of the species most sought after by keen growers.

ATHYRIUM FILIX-FEMINA VAR. FRIZELLIAE (the tatting fern). Hardy and deciduous in cool-temperature areas. The tiny, bead-like pinnae give the frond the appearance of a string of beads.

ATHYRIUM FILIX-FEMINA CV. VICTORIAE. Found growing wild in Britain in Victorian times and named for the Queen of the time. This is a beautiful and unusually formed fern with very narrow and dainty fronds which can be 1 m (3 ft) or more long. The pinnules form a criss-crossed pattern. Sporelings come true to parent plant form, but have evidently never equalled the parent plant in strength and vigour. It is considered hardy.

BLECHNUM

Water Ferns, Hard Ferns, Rib Ferns

This large genus of over 200 species is widespread throughout the world. Many of the species have pink new growth and form a distinct caudex with age.

BLECHNUM AUSTRALE. A terrestrial fern from the temperate to subtropical areas of Africa, South America and Madagascar. It is similar in appearance and habit to *B. orientale*. This fern will tolerate some sunlight, but requires plenty of moisture. It can be grown as a ground cover plant.

Blechnum gibbum

Blechnum brasiliense

BLECHNUM BRASILIENSE (Brazilian tree fern). The largest species of the *Blechnum* genus grows to about 1 m (3 ft) in height and has a tree fern-like character. The fronds can grow to a diameter of 1.5 m (5 ft). It is easy and not too demanding to grow, but must be kept well watered and the water kept off the fronds. It is a vigorous species, responding particularly to warmth and plenty of light, and will quickly outgrow its pot. Its natural habitat is the jungles of Brazil and Peru.

BLECHNUM BRASILIENSE CV. CRISPUM. This is a medium- to large-growing fern which is considered tender and requires plenty of protection. The coarse, green fronds are wavy and tinged with red when young.

BLECHNUM CAPENSE (palm-leaf fern). From the subalpine forests of New Zealand, the fronds of this species have two distinct forms — the barren fronds are glossy with finely serrated edges; and the fertile fronds are tall, narrow and covered with sori. It is very variable, the length of the fronds seeming to depend on environmental conditions. This fern is hardy, but grows best in humus-rich ground. It does not grow well in a pot.

BLECHNUM CARTILAGINEUM (bristle fern). A terrestrial plant found in eastern Australia and the Philippines. It has large, light green fronds with wavy edges; new growth is often pink. It is an easily grown plant which is hardy in a dry situation. Australian Aborigines used to eat the rhizome.

BLECHNUM DISCOLOR. Also from the subalpine forests of New Zealand, this *Blechnum* species is semi-hardy. It has narrow fronds varying in length from 30–100 cm (1–4 ft), is glossy green on top and greyish-green or cinnamon underneath. Young fronds are copper coloured. To cultivate successfully, this fern requires medium light and also needs to be kept moist.

BLECHNUM GIBBUM. A medium-sized fern. The deeply cut fronds form a closely knit spiral on top of the erect stem which coarsens and develops into a trunk with age. It is semi-tender, requiring medium light and a constantly moist soil. This fern makes an attractive potted plant.

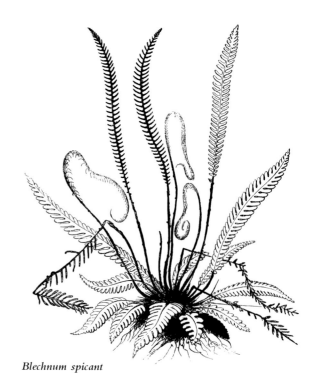

Blechnum spicant

BLECHNUM NUDUM (fishbone water fern). A common sight in the mountain areas of Victoria, Australia, where it forms dense colonies along stream or creek banks. The light green fronds are arranged from a central base in a symmetrical pattern. It is easily grown, but requires plenty of moisture.

BLECHNUM OCCIDENTALE (hammock fern). Native to the West Indies, Mexico, Central and South America; this small semi-tender member of the *Blechnum* genus has attractive reddish new growth. It needs plenty of light and to be kept moist, though this species is more tolerant than others of the genus to drier, exposed situations.

BLECHNUM PATERSONII (strap water fern). Found in eastern Australia, New Zealand and Fiji, this is a small species with strap-like fronds of variable shape. It grows easily in wet, shaded positions.

BLECHNUM PENNA-MARINA (alpine water fern). A hardy, dwarf, creeping species from eastern Australia, New Zealand, South America and sub-Antarctic islands. The fertile fronds are erect and the barren fronds spreading. It grows well in a pot.

BLECHNUM SPICANT (deer fern in the United States, hard fern, ladder fern). A dimorphic fern found widely throughout the Northern Hemisphere. The barren fronds are a glossy green with the pinnae set regularly like the teeth of a comb; the fertile fronds are longer. Again, the pinnae, though slimmer, are set in a regular pattern. It is a low-growing and hardy species that is tolerant of shade and easy to grown in temperate areas.

BLECHNUM WATSII (hard water fern). Native to the east coast of Australia, this fern can be found as the main ground cover in the moist mountainous areas of Victoria where it will climb the trunk of a tree fern. The new growth is pink. This species is easily grown with a little protection.

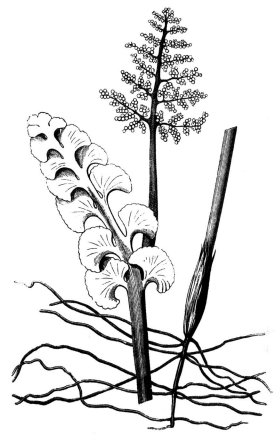

Botrychium lunaria

BOTRYCHIUM

Moonworts, Grape Ferns

A genus of about 25 species widely distributed throughout the world, though only a few species are cultivated. All moonworts have two fronds only — one barren and one fertile. The spores are carried in clusters like grapes above the single yellow-green, triangular fertile frond. The plant is also unique in that its fronds do not have the usual crosier-like development — it develops under the ground and is drawn out by the elongating stem.

BOTRYCHIUM LUNARIA (moonwort). This plant is included here because of its value as a fern curiosity and its association with the folklore that has grown around ferns, rather than for its value as a garden or potted plant. It is easy to cultivate once established, but needs some protection if grown in the open ground.

BOTRYCHIUM VIRGINIANUM (rattlesnake fern). A small, hardy, succulent species; the largest of the genus and one of the few *Botrychium* species cultivated. It is difficult to establish and is best transplanted with a large sod of the original earth to protect the fleshy roots. Thereafter it needs plenty of deep soil that is rich in leaf mould, medium light and plenty of moisture.

CAMPTOSORUS

A genus of two species of small, terrestrial ferns that inhabit limestone rocks in North America and northeast Asia.

CAMPTOSORUS RHIZOPHYLLUS (walking fern) alt. *Asplenium rhizophyllus.* A native to North America and northeast Asia, this is a small, hardy, terrestrial fern that thrives with its roots among limestone rocks. The long tapered fronds form new plants

Camptosorus rhizophyllus

when their tips rest on the soil and it will quickly colonise a sheltered rock garden. It is easily cared for and makes an attractive potted plant.

CETERACH

A small genus of three species of dwarf, xerophytic ferns found along the Mediterranean coast, and in central Europe, Britain, North Africa, west Asia and the Himalayas.

CETERACH OFFICINARUM (rustyback fern, scaly spleenwort in Britain — also known as *Asplenium ceterach*). A dwarf, xerophytic species native to Britain, Europe, west Asia and North Africa. It is very hardy and easy to grow, and is especially suited to wall and rock garden growing. The fronds have a leathery texture and are a light sage green. Silver scales, which turn brown as they mature, thickly clothe the undersides of the leaf. This fern can recover from dehydration even if it appears to have died.

CRYPTOGRAMMA

Rock Brakes

A genus of four species of small, coarse ferns which grow in rocky alpine and boreal areas (areas where the north winds blow) of Europe, Asia and America.

CRYPTOGRAMMA CRISPA (parsley fern). A small, hardy, dimorphic fern which strongly resembles parsley in colour and form. It is difficult to cultivate unless the ground is kept continually moist and the fronds are in light shade. It will not tolerate lime, but grows well in rock gardens, like its natural habitat, the alpine areas of the Northern Hemisphere.

Culcita dubia

CULCITA

A genus of about nine species from tropical and subtropical areas of the Southern Hemisphere.

CULCITA DUBIA (common ground fern, rainbow fern, false bracken). One of the most common ferns growing wild in eastern Australia where its large, yellow-green fronds clothe the sides of roads and streams. While easily cultivated in open garden situations, it needs room to spread.

CYRTOMIUM

Holly Ferns

This is a genus of medium-growing ferns with tough, leathery foliage. It grows naturally in the tropics and subtropics.

CYRTOMIUM FALCATUM (house holly fern in the United States, Japanese holly fern in Britain). This species is used extensively as an indoor plant because

Cyrtomium falcatum

of its medium size, attractive shiny green leaves, hardiness, and its tolerance of direct morning and late afternoon sunlight. Both this, and its cultivar Rochfordianum, need medium to high light and moist conditions and should be kept on the dry side of moist over winter. Both plants are tolerant of drier, exposed positions if they are watered regularly until established.

CYRTOMIUM FALCATUM CV. BUTTERFIELDII (Butterfield fern, Japanese holly fern). Similar to the following cultivar, but with slightly smaller leaf form. It is tolerant of low light and humidity.

CYRTOMIUM FALCATUM CV. ROCHFORDIANUM (Rochford fern). This cultivar has a more pronounced holly-shaped leaf and is easy to grow both indoors and outdoors, requiring the same light and moisture conditions as its parent species (see p. 129).

CYSTOPTERIS

Bladder Ferns

The ferns of this genus are mostly small and delicate. Only a few are in general cultivation where they are suited to a shaded rock garden. The common name comes from the inflated, hood-like indusium.

CYSTOPTERIS BULBIFERA (berry bladder fern, bulblet bladder fern). A medium-growing species, though the length of the fronds may vary. Bulblets form at the junction of pinna to rachis and develop into new plants. A native of North America, it is a hardy plant and grows best in a moist to wet situation.

CYSTOPTERIS FRAGILIS (brittle bladder fern, fragile bladder fern). A fern widely distributed throughout the world. Small and hardy, it likes low light and shade. It is suitable for a terrarium.

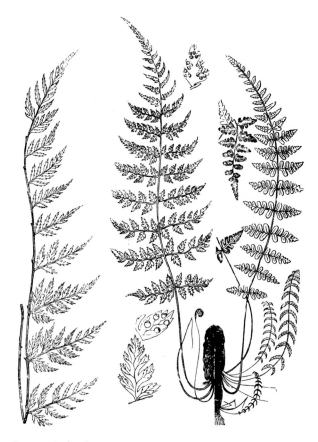

Cystopteris fragilis

DAVALLIA

Hare's Foot Ferns, Rabbit's Foot Ferns, Squirrel's Foot Ferns

The *Davallia* genus is familiar to most gardeners. The species are small- to medium-growing epiphytes with long, creeping rhizomes covered in soft scales, which grow naturally in tropical areas of Asia and Australia. The fronds of each species are fairly similar — some are broad and deeply dissected, some coarse and some very finely divided. They are all triangular in shape and supported on wiry stems. Growing in the wild in association with staghorn and elkhorn ferns, their rhizomes sometimes penetrate and destroy these plants.

Many of the species are deciduous, the fronds turning golden yellow before dropping. In ideal growing conditions, the old fronds may linger so that their deciduous habit is hardly noticeable. If the new fronds appear before the old have dropped, it is a good idea to remove them to make way for new growth. These plants will also drop their leaves in times of low humidity or drought, which makes them a hardy species.

Being epiphytes, *Davallia* species are ideal for hanging baskets. When well established, several plants will cover the outside of a basket entirely, turning it into an attractive ball of fronds for most of the year. Even without the fronds, a well-established hanging basket makes an attractive furry mass of criss-crossed rhizomes. Planted in the ground among rocks, these ferns form a dense ground cover.

If the creeping rhizomes become too tangled, it is best to break up the clumps, discarding the old, dead portions, and replant the portions with growing tips. The rhizomes should be planted so that they are resting *on* the soil surface. Put several of the new plants in and around the sides of a basket lined with moss, paperbark, or carpet underfelt, or a basket made of tree fern wood. The roots quickly establish in these soft media. The new growing tips on the rhizomes can be tied down with raffia or wire.

The *Davallia* species make ideal potted and hanging basket plants for the house as they are able to tolerate slightly drier air than most ferns because their rhizomes store moisture. Their soil should be kept on the dry side of moist so that the rhizome does not rot. Propagation is by division of the rhizomes, or by spores sown in the spring.

DAVALLIA CANARIENSIS (Canary Island Hare's foot fern). This is a slow-growing, but long-lived fern with finely divided, broad fronds and a pendulous habit which makes it suitable for a hanging basket or elevated pot. It is native to the temperate to subtropical areas of Portugal, Spain and the Canary Islands.

Davallia canariensis

DAVALLIA DENTICULATA (toothed davallia). A hardy, but frost-tender species from Australia and Asia. In its natural habitat, this fern sometimes grows in very exposed positions. It has deeply divided fronds and a thick rhizome covered in light brown scales.

DAVALLIA FEJEENSIS. A small- to medium-growing tender species from the tropical islands of Fiji. It is tolerant of most light conditions. The soil should be kept on the dry side of moist. Layers of delicate lacy fronds make this an attractive hanging basket or potted plant.

DAVALLIA FEJEENSIS CV. MAJOR. This is similar to *D. fejeensis*, but larger. This is a popular but tender species, tolerant of most light conditions. Soil should be kept on the dry side of moist.

DAVALLIA FEJEENSIS CV. PLUMOSA (plume davallia). The most delicate and finely cut of the *Davallia* genus. Small to medium growing, it is tolerant of most light conditions. Soil should be kept on the dry side of moist.

DAVALLIA MARIESII (ball fern). A hardy species from Japan with shiny green fronds. The creeping rhizome is covered with grey-brown, silky scales with white silky growing tips.

DAVALLIA PYXIDATA. A native Australian species, small growing and hardy.

DAVALLIA TRICHOMANOIDES (squirrel's foot fern). Native to Southeast Asia, Sri Lanka, Malaysia and Indonesia, this is easily grown, medium-sized, with graceful arching fronds and nut brown scales on the rhizome. A little frost tender, but tolerant of morning and late afternoon sunlight. Suitable for a rock garden as it likes to be kept on the dry side of moist. Its fronds look attractive in a hanging basket.

DENNSTAEDTIA
Cup Ferns

The genus is found throughout the world and is considered rather primitive. The species all have triangular, finely dissected fronds.

DENNSTAEDTIA DAVALLIOIDES (lacy ground fern). A primitive species endemic to Australia, commonly cultivated as a hardy, attractive pot or garden plant. In an ideal cool, protected situation it can become a nuisance in the garden.

Davallia pyxidata

Dennstaedtia davallioides

DENNSTAEDTIA PUNTILOBULA (hay-scented fern). An adaptable species from North America with long, delicate, tapering fronds and new growth covered in white hairs. The pleasant smell of new mown hay comes from minute glands on the undersides of mature fronds. It is so adaptable that it is considered a weed in some temperature areas.

DOODIA

Rasp Ferns, Hacksaw Ferns

A worldwide genus of small- to medium-growing terrestrial ferns. They are hardy and thrive in cultivation, but are slow growing. The fronds are long and tapering at both ends, often harsh to the touch. New growth is reddish.

DOODIA ASPERA (prickly rasp fern). From Australia, where it is common in the eastern states, this fern is hardy and easy to cultivate. New fronds are an attractive bright pink. The mature fronds are rough and grow up to 60 cm (2 ft) in length.

DOODIA CAUDATA (small rasp fern). From Australia and New Zealand, this is a slender delicate species with dimorphic sterile and fertile fronds. Some fronds extend into a long tail up to 30 cm (1 ft) in

Doodia media

length. These fronds tend to weep gracefully, thus making this species ideal for a hanging basket. Maoris used this fern as a source of perfume. Easily grown, but slow, it needs some shelter in the open ground.

DOODIA MEDIA (common rasp fern in Australia, hacksaw fern in the United States). A small- to medium-growing species commonly cultivated. It is slightly tender, requires plenty of light and to be kept on the dry side of moist. New fronds are an attractive purplish-red. This is an easily cultivated, but slow-growing species.

DORYOPTERIS

This is a genus of small ferns, mainly from tropical America, with maple leaf-like fronds borne on the end of long, shiny stipes.

Doodia aspera

DORYOPTERIS PEDATA VAR. PALMATA (hand fern). A small, slightly tender species which is commonly cultivated. It needs warmth and protection, medium light conditions and some humidity.

DRYNARIA

Oak Leaf Ferns

A genus of about 20 species of medium- to large-growing ferns from tropical parts of Asia. Generally tender. Individual plants form two types of leaves — humus collecting oak-like, and long and divided.

DRYNARIA QUERCIFOLIA (also known as *Polypodium quercifolia*, *Phymatodes quercifolia* and *Polypodium sylvaticum*). A tender species from Malaysia, India, southern China, Fiji and northern Queensland, Australia. It is an attractive species with distinctly dimorphic fronds. In parts of Asia the fern has been used as an astringent and to treat typhoid fever and colds. It needs protection in winter in temperate areas, high humidity and well-drained soil. The rhizome should not be planted too deeply and should be anchored firmly in order to establish a new plant. This species grows best in a large hanging basket or pot.

DRYNARIA VULGARIS. See *Phymatodes scolopendrium*.

DRYOPTERIS

Shield Ferns, Buckler Ferns

A worldwide genus of generally hardy ferns for cultivation. Mostly medium-sized plants with thick erect rhizomes and fronds forming a crown.

DRYOPTERIS AUSTRIACA SPINULOSA (broad shield fern, broad buckler fern, toothed wood fern — also *D. dilatata*, *D. spinulosa* var. *dilatata*). A robust, hardy woodland fern found in Europe, Asia, North America, Greenland and Japan, with finely dissected fronds which are used commercially by florists.

DRYOPTERIS DILATATA. See *D. austriaca spinulosa*.

DRYOPTERIS ERYTHROSORA (autumn fern, Japanese shield fern). A hardy and attractive species with glossy, coppery pink new growth. A native of Japan, China and the Philippines, this species will grow in shady situations or in areas of morning and late afternoon sun.

DRYOPTERIS FILIX-MAS (male fern). A hardy species of the Northern Hemisphere that has feathered and

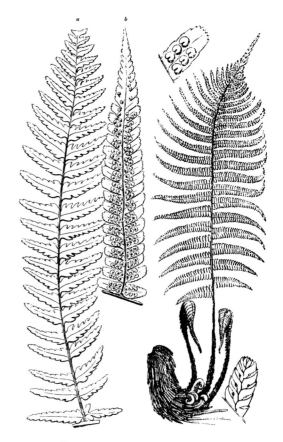

Dryopteris filix-mas

crested foliage. It is found growing wild thoughout Britain, but is rare in North America. The plant is very variable and has given rise to many varieties which are universally cultivated. The common name male fern comes from its robust appearance, and dates from Chaucer's time.

DRYOPTERIS MARGINALIS (marginal shield fern, marginal buckler fern). A hardy shade-tolerant species that is native to North America. It forms a short root stock and a single crop of long, dark blue-green fronds.

DRYOPTERIS PHEGOPTERIS. See *Thelypteris phegopteris*.

DRYOPTERIS SPINULOSA VAR. DILATATA. See *D. austriaca spinulosa*.

DRYOPTERIS THELYPTERIS. See *Thelypteris palustris*.

Gleichenia circinata semi-vestita

GLEICHENIA
Coral Ferns, Umbrella Ferns

A small genus of about ten species which grow in many and varied habitats, usually with their roots in boggy or damp soil and their scrambling fronds in full sunlight. The genus is instantly recognisable by the unusual fronds which branch and rebranch. Individual species may grow and cover an area of hundreds of metres or feet, forming an impenetrable, tangled mass. On the whole, the genus is hardy, but difficult to transplant and slow to re-establish.

GLEICHENIA DICARPA (pouched coral fern, tangle fern). A common, widespread species found in Australia, New Zealand and Southeast Asia. It is easy to cultivate if the roots are kept very moist and the fronds are in some sunlight. It is very difficult to transplant a large species, so it is best to concentrate on establishing small plants.

GLEICHENIA DICARPA MICROPHYLLA (scrambling coral fern, umbrella fern, parasol fern). This is a spreading, strong-growing species that forms large masses, often weighing down low-growing shrubs and other ferns in its natural habitat along stream or creek banks in Australia, New Zealand and Southeast Asia. It is easy to cultivate if the roots are kept very moist and the fronds are exposed to some sunlight.

GRAMMITIS

A genus of approximately 150 small epiphytes and lithophytes which grow in tropical and subtropical parts of the world.

GRAMMITIS AUSTRALIS. See *G. billardieri*.

GRAMMITIS BILLARDIERI (finger fern — also known as *Grammitis australis*). This species is native to Australia, New Zealand, South Africa and South America where it grows among rocks. Long oblong fronds can grow up to 16 cm (7 in) and give the plant its common name. It is difficult to cultivate.

GYMNOCARPIUM

Oak Ferns

Small- to medium-growing ferns from the temperate areas of the world. The fronds, on slender stipes, are spaced well apart on the long creeping rhizome.

GYMNOCARPIUM DRYOPTERIS (common oak fern — also known as *Polypodium dryopteris*). A worldwide species that has been reclassified many times over the past few decades. The plant is very small with bright, golden green, slender stipes and delicate, triple-branched, golden green fronds. It is common as a ground cover in eastern North America. The new, unfurling fronds look intriguingly like a pawn broker's sign. An ideal and hardy garden plant, suited to rock gardens, it needs plenty of room to spread.

HELMINTHOSTACHYS

A genus of one species that grows throughout Southeast Asia.

HELMINTHOSTACHYS ZEYLANICA (flowering fern). The palmate sterile fronds borne on a long stipe; and the fleshy, fertile frond borne on an offshoot above the sterile fronds give the species the appearance of a flowering plant — hence the common name. The creeping rhizome is eaten as a vegetable in Malaysia. This species is easily grown if protected from frost.

HISTIOPTERIS

A small genus of large robust plants.

HISTIOPTERIS INCISA (bat's wing fern, oak fern). A terrestrial creeping fern with large, pale green fronds, the tips of which grow continuously. It grows best in a cool, moist situation in the ground or in a pot. It is widespread throughout Australia and in some areas it is regarded as a pest.

Histiopteris incisa

HUMATA

A genus of about 40 species spread throughout Southeast Asia, Polynesia, Malaysia and Madagascar. All are small- to medium-growing epiphytic ferns. This genus is closely related to the *Davallia* genus, but generally, individual plants are smaller.

HUMATA TYERMANNII (bear's foot fern). A slow-growing, semi-tender species from central China which needs plenty of light. This fern grows well and looks attractive in a hanging basket. The soil should be kept on the dry side of moist. This is a suitable species for a rock garden.

HYPOLEPIS

This genus consists of medium- to large-sized, rapidly growing, creeping ground ferns with mostly finely divided, triangular fronds. There are about 45 species of *Hypolepis*, with a wide distribution throughout the world.

HYPOLEPIS MILLEFOLIUM. A species from New Zealand which has what are considered the most finely cut fronds of any fern. It is easy to grow, but prefers lime-free conditions and protection from extreme cold.

HYPOLEPIS TENUIFOLIA. A large, semi-hardy species from Australia and New Zealand which is easy to grow. It has pale stems that are covered with soft, white hairs.

Lastreopsis hispida

Humata tyermannii

LASTREOPSIS

A widely distributed genus of handsome ferns with broad, lacy fronds. Mostly medium-sized, terrestrial plants.

LASTREOPSIS HISPIDA (bristly shield fern). Native to New Zealand, it is a little tender and should be protected from frost and kept thoroughly moist, but perfectly drained. A beautiful fern that is worth the extra care needed to cultivate it.

LASTREOPSIS MICROSORA (creeping shield fern). A vigorous Australian species, dainty looking and semi-tender but easy to cultivate. It is tolerant of morning and late afternoon sunlight.

LEPTOPTERIS

Crepe Ferns

A small genus of about 60 species from mostly tropical parts of the world. They have filmy fronds borne in a whorl on the crown rather like a tree fern, and a woody trunk up to 1 m (3 ft) high. They are delicate ferns which require the same conditions as filmy ferns — i.e. shade, plenty of moisture and high humidity. The species *Leptopteris superba* and *L. hymenophylloides* are listed in old fern books as members of the *Todea* and *Osmunda* genera, to which they are closely related.

LEPTOPTERIS HYMENOPHYLLOIDES. A species native to New Zealand that is difficult, but rewarding, to cultivate. It requires shade, very high humidity, shelter and moist conditions. The fern may grow in a cool or unheated greenhouse as long as the humidity is kept high — in such conditions the fronds may reach 60 cm (2 ft) in length and 45 cm (18 in) in width, and old specimens may develop a short trunk.

LEPTOPTERIS SUPERBA (Prince of Wales feather). This New Zealand species is considered one of the most beautiful ferns in cultivation; like *L. hymenophylloides*, it is very demanding to cultivate and requires the same conditions. The prothallus is long-lived and hardy, but the sporophyte is slow to establish. Fine specimens of the species and *L. wilkesiana* can be seen in Kew Gardens, London.

LYGODIUM

A widespread genus of about 40 species whose structure is complex and differs greatly from that of

Leptopteris superba

Lygodium japonicum

other ferns. The species are vigorous climbing plants which grow naturally throughout the rainforest regions of the world.

LYGODIUM JAPONICUM (Japanese climbing fern). This species, with yellow-green leaves, is widespread thoughout Asia and Australasia. In a sheltered, frost-free position it will twine vigorously and daintily up a support or trail from a hanging basket, looking more like a vine than a fern. It is easy to grow, but good drainage is essential and there should be ample humidity in the atmosphere for the fern to look its best. It is tolerant of morning and late afternoon sunlight.

LYGODIUM PALMATUM (Hartford fern). A dimorphic, climbing fern native to North America where it grows in woodland areas. It is tolerant of low light conditions, but is semi-tender so, if grown outside, should be protected from frost. The soil should be deep and rich. This fern should have strong supports on which to climb. It is suited to growing in a hanging basket.

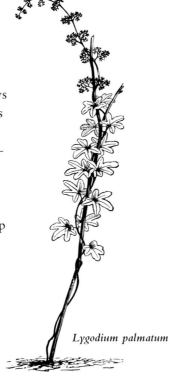

Lygodium palmatum

MARATTIA

A genus of about 60 species of primitive ferns from the tropical areas of Australia, Southeast Asia, Polynesia and South Africa. The species are thick and coarse, and closely resemble the *Angiopteris* genus. They are readily cultivated.

MARATTIA FRAXINEA. See *M. salicina*.

MARATTIA SALICINA (potato fern — also known as *M. fraxinea*). A strong-growing, large creeping fern from tropical areas of Queensland, Australia, and Southeast Asia. The fronds have fleshy stipes and may grow up to 4 m (14 ft) long in a protected situation. The plant is hardy to frost when mature. The starchy rhizomes are eaten by Maoris in New Zealand. The tissues turn purple when cut.

MATTEUCCIA

This is genus of dimorphic, medium-sized ferns from the northern temperate areas of the world.

MATTEUCCIA STRUTHIOPTERIS (ostrich fern). A large, strong and fast-growing, easily cultivated fern which is native to Europe and North Africa. The common name comes from the smaller fertile frond-carrying pinnae that form in clusters of tufts. The species will grow in wet or boggy soils. The fiddleheads are edible (see p. 27).

MICROSORIUM

A large genus of epiphytes growing on tree trunks in the wild. It is closely related to the *Polypodium* genus and the species are often referred to as such.

MICROSORIUM DIVERSIFOLIUM alt. *Phymatosorus diversifolius* (kangaroo fern). An easily grown, creeping species from Australia and New Zealand with semi-weeping, extremely variable fronds. It grows well in a pot if given good drainage and a support to cling to. This fern is also an attractive hanging basket plant.

MICROSORIUM SCANDENS (fragrant fern — also known as *Polypodium scandens*). A subtropical fern, native to the southeast of Australia and most of New Zealand, which has been reclassified many times. The semi-weeping fronds are extremely variable. It is a scrambling fern which, in the wild, almost smothers the upper parts of tree fern trunks and the branches of low trees. The common name comes from the distinctive, but faint, aroma of the fresh fronds — it is more pronounced if the frond is dried and crushed. It is easy to cultivate, tolerates low light conditions, and is easy to propagate from spores or by division of the rhizome.

NEPHROLEPIS

Fishbone Ferns, Boston Ferns, Sword Ferns, Lace Ferns

This is a widespread genus of epiphytic ferns which are, on the whole, vigorous, tolerant of dry air and high temperatures, and easy to cultivate. If these ferns are grown in a pot, it is essential that the soil is well aerated and watering is carried out carefully. It is important that the foliage should not stay wet because it will become matted and the fronds will be lost or disfigured. The soil must be kept on the dry side of moist during the colder months when the plant is not growing. The fronds look more lush if the plant is kept slightly rootbound, fertilised regulary and if there is ample humidity in the atmosphere. An occasional yellowing of the old fronds is quite natural in a plant that is growing vigorously. The fronds should be trimmed regularly to allow light and air to reach the new growth.

Plantlets that revert to plain fishbone-type foliage should be removed as they are vigorous and can overwhelm more attractive foliage.

Members of the *Nephrolepis* genus have long, slender scaly stems (stolons) which produce new plants when they touch the soil. New plants that form on the stolons may be divided from the parent plant after they have produced two or more fronds. They should be placed in small pots that just contain the rootball. The species can also be propagated easily by division, meristem culture and spores (except the true Boston fern, *N. exaltata* var. *bostoniensis*, and its derivatives, which do not produce spores).

Most *Nephrolepis* species and cultivars are considered hardy enough for the amateur grower to be able to cultivate them inside the house, in the unheated greenhouse or outside in sheltered areas.

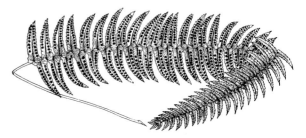

Nephrolepis cordifolia frond

NEPHROLEPIS CORDIFOLIA (tuber sword fern, common fishbone fern in southern parts of Australia, herringbone fern). This species is widely distributed throughout the world from the tropics to the subtropics, where it colonises freely. The fronds are up to 1 m (3 ft) long, narrow and a dull green. The pinnae are narrow and well spaced at the top and bottom of each frond, but tend to overlap in the centre. This species is distinguished from the species *N. exaltata* by its oval, brown scaly tubers on sub-terranean stolons. It is hardy, fast growing, very easy to cultivate and will tolerate long periods of cold and full sunlight. It can be propagated by means of the tubers, which form new growth if separated from the

Nephrolepis cordifolia var. *plumosa*

parent plant. The variety *N. cordifolia* var. *plumosa* is also easy to cultivate. Its long and attractive fronds are displayed particularly well in a hanging basket.

NEPHROLEPIS EXALTATA (sword fern, fishbone fern). Found in temperate and tropical parts of Asia, Africa, Australia and the Americas, this species was introduced to cultivation from Jamaica in 1793 and quickly became a popular greenhouse plant with over 100 cultivars recorded to date. The fronds, which are larger and longer than the fronds of *N. cordifolia*, are generally fairly stiff, dark green and will grow indefinitely. Growth is softer and more arching if the plant is cultivated in the shade, and warmth and humidity are provided.

NEPHROLEPIS EXALTATA VAR. BOSTONIENSIS (Boston fern). This fern, descendant of the sword or fishbone fern *N. exaltata*, has an interesting history. In 1895, a florist near Boston found among his sword ferns a new variety with softer, longer, more graceful foliage, and many more leaves. It was greatly admired and was soon cultivated widely. The mutation — not due to hybridisation evidently, but to a change of genes — went wild and, almost simultaneously, there appeared among the many thousands of Boston ferns in widely separate localities, a half dozen strikingly different plants whose leaves were ruffled and frilled in multiple divisions. A constant succession of new and improved varieties then followed so that more than 200 named varieties have come from this one extraordinary fern. At least 100 of these have been recognised as different varieties.

Other commonly and easily grown *N. exaltata* cultivars are: cv. Verona, which has yellow-green, lacy fronds; cv. Childsii, which has luxuriant, massed leaflets; cv. Gretnae, cv. Rooseveltii and cv. Randpholii, all of which have very long fronds; cv. Elegantissima and cv. Whitmanii, the very lacy members of the family; cv. Hilsii, with vigorous, coarse-textured, pendulous fronds, each of which has a variation of dark to light green and wavy leaflets; and cv. Smithii and cv. Susi Wong, which are the extremely finely divided varieties.

Nephrolepis exaltata cv. Susi Wong

ONOCLEA

Sensitive Ferns

This is a genus of coarse-looking terrestrial ferns from North America. These ferns are dimorphic with broad, triangular barren fronds and fertile fronds like clusters of beads.

ONOCLEA SENSIBILIS (bead fern, American oak fern). One of the most common ferns in North America. Very variable and so adaptable and fast growing that it can become a nuisance in the garden. The individual pinnae sometimes resemble an oak leaf, hence one common name. (The common name of the genus comes from its sensitivity to early frosts). It is hardy, but should be kept on the wet side of moist as it grows naturally in wet or boggy soil.

Onoclea sensibilis

OPHIOGLOSSUM

Adder's Tongue Ferns

This worldwide genus is included here because it is an interesting rather than a cultivated fern, and for its historical and mystical associations (see pp. 28, 30).

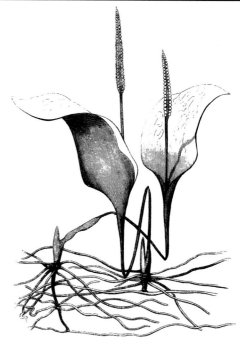

Ophioglossum vulgatum

There are usually only two fronds, with the fertile frond growing from the base of the stalk-like barren frond.

OPHIOGLOSSUM ENGLEMANII, OPHIOGLOSSUM LUSITANICUM and **OPHIOGLOSSUM VULGATUM**. All are difficult to grow and seldom seen out of their natural habitats.

OSMUNDA

Royal Ferns

Distributed throughout the world, the *Osmunda* genus consists of medium- to large-growing ferns, some of which form majestic crowns of fronds. In their natural habitat, they are found in damp places where there is deep rich soil. The coarse, fibrous roots made by these ferns are collected and used as a growing medium and compost by orchid growers. All species will grow in areas of morning and late afternoon sunlight.

OSMUNDA CINNAMOMEA. A hardy, shade-tolerant, large-growing, North American fern that must be kept thoroughly and constantly moist. The species is dimorphic; its name comes from the fertile fronds, which are dark green when young and a bright cinnamon-brown when ripe.

Osmunda cinnamomea

Osmunda claytoniana

OSMUNDA CLAYTONIANA (interrupted fern). A large, hardy species which is tolerant of low light, but which requires constantly moist and acid soil. The common name comes from the spore-bearing pinnae which are shorter than, and grow between, normal pinnae. The spores of this fern remain fertile for a few days only.

OSMUNDA REGALIS (royal fern). One of the largest of the terrestrial ferns of the temperate world, it is hardy and shade tolerant, and requires constantly and thoroughly moist and acid soil conditions. It thrives in boggy situations. The fronds change colour attractively in autumn (fall). A common misnomer is 'flowering fern', which comes from the resemblance of the fertile fronds to seedheads of flowering plants.

Osmunda regalis

In New Zealand, *O. regalis* has escaped and has colonised in swamps around Auckland. It was a fashionable fern in Victorian times when the English countryside was almost denuded of it.

PARACETERACH

A genus of a single species which is found only in the northern parts of Queensland in Australia.

PARACETERACH MUELLERI. A small fern found growing among rocks in northern Queensland, Australia. It is not commonly cultivated, but is interesting because of its ability to resist drought by curling its fronds, and to recover completely after rain. It needs warmth and protection to grow well.

Paraceterach muelleri

PELLAEA

Brakes, Cliff Brakes, Rock Brakes

This is a genus of mainly small-growing, xerophytic ferns which grow among rocks and are adapted to survive in dry climates. The fronds are usually fishbone-like in formation and the developing crosiers like a shepherd's crook. It is a large genus, which grows in dry, subtropical areas of the world.

Pellaea rotundifolia

PELLAEA ATROPURPUREA (purple cliff brake). A small, hardy species from North America which grows well in a pot or in a rock garden with some exposure to sunlight. The fronds are blue-green and the stems purple-brown. Plants should be kept on the dry side of moist. It is tolerant of limestone conditions.

PELLAEA FALCATA (sickle fern, Australian cliff brake). An easily grown, fairly hardy Australian species with elongated, shiny green fronds which bear neatly arranged pinnae. Vernation is non-circinate. Plants should be kept on the dry side of moist and will tolerate some sun.

PELLAEA ROTUNDIFOLIA (New Zealand cliff brake, button fern). A small-growing, spreading, xerophytic fern that is fairly hardy. Button-shaped pinnae make it attractive and popular as a cultivated plant. This species should be kept on the dry side of moist.

PELLAEA VIRIDIS VAR. VIRIDIS (green cliff brake). A delicate and slightly tender species with thin lance-like pinnae. It comes from subtropical areas of North America. One of the largest members of this genus, this fern needs plenty of light and should be kept on the dry side of moist.

PHLEBODIUM

A genus of only two species from tropical America, recently differentiated from the *Polypodium* genus.

PHLEBODIUM AUREUM (golden polypody — also known as *Polypodium aureum*). A large-growing species with deeply cut leaves up to 25 cm (10 in) across and 40 cm (16 in) long. The rhizome is thick and densely covered with orange-brown fur. The fronds are a soft blue-green and are displayed to advantage in a hanging basket or pot. This species is easy to cultivate, semi-tender, tolerant of some sunlight in mornings and late afternoons, and dry or exposed situations.

PHYLLITIS

Hart's-Tongue Ferns

This genus consists of small, evergreen ferns with tongue-shaped fronds found in temperate areas of the Northern Hemisphere. Individual species in cultivation are classified under the genus *Asplenium*.

PHYLLITIS SCOLOPENDRIUM. See *Asplenium scolopendrium*.

PHYMATODES

This is a small genus of ferns, which are similar in structure to those of the *Microsorium* genus. Several species have been moved from one genus to another over the past few decades.

PHYMATODES QUERCIFOLIA. See *Drynaria quercifolia*.

PHYMATODES SCOLOPENDRIUM (wart fern — also *Drynaria vulgaris*, *Polypodium scolopendrium*). This fern, which is found in subtropical areas of the world, has been classified under several genera and assigned many different names. The rhizome is creeping, a waxy green, and irregularly covered with dark brown, stiff, hair-like scales. The deeply lobed fronds are a dark emerald green, and the fertile fronds have 'wart-like' protuberances on their upper surface due to the deeply depressed sori on the underside. It is a medium-growing, easily cultivated plant, which requires a loose growing medium rich in humus and good drainage, good light and thorough watering.

Phymatodes scolopendrium

PITYROGRAMMA

Goldback Ferns, Silverback Ferns

Dense yellow and white powder on the back of the fronds make this xerophytic genus very attractive. The species are small to medium growing, tender, because they come from the African and American tropics, but tolerant of morning and late afternoon sunlight. The genus is now widespread throughout the world as many species have naturalised.

PITYROGRAMMA AUSTROAMERICANA (gold fern — also known as *P. chrysophylla*). A species originally native to South America and the West Indies. However, like the silver fern, it has naturalised in many countries. It is sometimes called the 'king of the gold ferns'. A dense rich gold or creamy white, waxy powder forms on the unfurling crosiers and the undersides of the fronds. It is a tender plant, medium-growing, and only thrives with plenty of light and moist to dry soil conditions.

PITYROGRAMMA CALOMELANOS (silver fern). A species native to South America which has naturalised in many countries of the world so that its origins have almost been lost. The fronds are fine and lacy, and the undersides are covered with a silver-white powder. The plant is tender, and needs plenty of light, and moist to dry conditions to thrive.

PITYROGRAMMA CHRYSOPHYLLA. See *P. austroamericana*.

PITYROGRAMMA HYBRIDA. A successful hybrid of *P. austroamericana* and *P. calomelanos*, which has pale yellow-green fronds with gold powdering on the undersides. It is considered more beautiful than both of its parents, and more luxuriant and graceful. This fern is semi-hardy and the fronds are relatively tolerant of dry air, but the roots must be kept moist and the plant repotted frequently to accommodate the strong-growing root system.

Pityrogramma austroamericana

PLATYCERIUM

Staghorn, Elkhorn and Moosehorn Ferns

This is a genus of lithophytic or epiphytic ferns whose shape, form and habit are unique in the fern world. There are about 17 species found mainly in the tropics of South America, Africa, Asia and Australia. Several cultivars are in existence. They vary in size from the small *P. madagascariense* which is approximately 30 cm (12 in) overall, to the giant *P. wilhelminae-reginae* with a shield over 2 m (7 ft) across and fertile fronds that hang to almost 2 m (7 ft). The different species are often

Platycerium superbum

hard to identify as some plants may take from five to seven years to produce their first fertile fronds, which even then are often variable.

The *Platycerium* species are dimorphic plants. The flattened sterile fronds are at the back and base of the plant, and go brown and brittle with age so that often only a skeleton remains. New fronds have a dense wax-like appearance and feel, and gradually spread plate-like foliage over the base of the plant. The fertile fronds, which hang in front of the plant, are erect and multi-branched, and resemble the antlers of a deer. They are a delicate green and their tips are covered with a downy pubescence of a paler green. In some species, as the fertile fronds mature, they take on a bluish tint, and the lower back portion, which is covered densely with spore cases, looks like brown velvet.

Platycerium species grow naturally in the rainforest areas of the world where, high up in the trees, they become entangled among vines and other climbing plants. They also grow on old logs, rocks and fallen trees, feeding on the decaying matter of their host, or wrapped around the fibrous trunks of

other ferns in a relationship that is of mutual benefit. They are not parasites; there is no such species in the fern world. Their aerial roots get food from the decaying matter trapped in their own leaf systems or the bark and crevices of their host. Because rainwater collects in this humus, they are resistant to long periods of drought. They are well designed to 'trap' their food: the huge nest leaves at the back of the plant are shield-like and tilted outwards at their top, trapping and directing falling debris to the depths of the plant where it breaks down into a rich humus and readily available plant food.

The *Platycerium* species grow naturally on trees with non-shedding bark, like those of the fig, cedar, sassafras and coachwood families, and occasionally on rocks. In cultivation, they can be grown on boards fixed to walls or trees, or fixed directly to a tree that does not shed its bark. Copper or galvanised wires that will not rust should be used to attach a plant to a tree. Do not wrap the wires around the tree's trunk because they may cause damage if they cut into the cambium layer just beneath the bark. Fix the wire to nails driven straight into the tree's wood. Magnificent old staghorn and elkhorn ferns, fixed in this way originally, are often seen wrapped right around the trunk of a supporting tree so that all signs of their support have long since disappeared.

If grown on a board support, it is important that the board be made of stout hardwood and that the plant be fixed firmly so movement will not dislodge the roots. This may be done by nailing the fern to the board with long nails, after first driving the nail through an improvised washer made of leather or rubber. Make sure that the base of the plant is secure because it is from here that the anchoring roots will develop. The top of the plant should project forward slightly so that decayed matter is directed to the roots. Nature has designed the *Platycerium* genus perfectly to be self-sufficient, so you should understand it to grow it successfully. Pack a generous amount of sphagnum moss between the fern and the board to give the roots shelter, until the natural fibrous matter accumulates. Organic matter and water is all that is needed to maintain the plant — no soil is necessary.

If the fern is placed so that it is growing away from trees or in a place where organic matter will not collect naturally, feed it with handfuls of well-rotted leaf mould and old cow manure. Tuck this food well down, behind the old nest leaves. An old banana skin is a rich source of nitrogen if fed to the plant several times a year. Do not be tempted to use chemical fertilisers in powdered form as any undissolved granules may collect in the joints of the old fronds, burning them and creating a situation in which fungus will thrive.

In the treetops, the epiphytes receive plenty of the available rainfall, and this water drains through the aerial roots quickly. To recreate these conditions in a garden, the ferns should be watered thoroughly, but not constantly. A state of constant wetness at the base of the plant, behind the shield fronds, encourages

rot. Use the hose to water thoroughly all over, or, if the plant is small enough, take it down and soak it, supporting board and all, until both are saturated. Do not be tempted to sprinkle the plant every time the garden is watered as this will keep it constantly wet; but on a hot day mist the plant with a fine spray from the hose to increase the humidity. Several days after a thorough watering, the outer fronds may feel dry to the touch, but check before watering again by pressing firmly with the fingers on the base of the lower fronds. If water oozes out, the plant is wet enough and should be left for a few more days. Some growers actually wait until the fertile fronds look limp before watering.

It is very important to see that overhead eaves or hanging baskets do not drip constantly onto epiphytic ferns, as this will, once again, encourage constant wetness.

These ferns may be propagated by cutting established clumps into sections when a number of plantlets have formed on their bases. Buds or young plantlets, bearing several shield fronds, may be removed safely from the parent plant and mounted individually on boards, or planted out in pots. Use a sharp knife to cut beneath and around the oldest shield frond of the young plant. If possible, take a small section of the base fronds of the parent plant with the section. All the ferns of the *Platycerium* genus, except *P. veitchii*, are also easily propagated by spores.

PLATYCERIUM ALCICORNE. See *P. bifurcatum*.

PLATYCERIUM BIFURCATUM (common staghorn in the United States, elkhorn in Australia — also known as *P. alcicorne*). A species native to Australia (where it is the most common and most widespread species), Lord Howe Island, New Caledonia and Papua New Guinea. The kidney-shaped, deep green shield fronds grow tightly pressed against layers of old fronds which quickly turn brown. The fertile, pendulous fronds branch into two or three parts and hang lower

Platycerium bifurcatum

Platycerium superbum

PLATYCERIUM SUPERBUM (staghorn in Australia, elkhorn or moosehorn in the United States — also known as *P. grande*). Until recently, this was known as *P. grande*, a species found in the Philippines, but it is now known to be a different species. The shield fronds are fan-shaped, and divided at irregular intervals at the top. Major veins show attractively through the fronds. Fertile fronds are light green, thin, narrow and pendulous. They fork at less than half their length and the spores are carried in a large patch at the point of the first fork. This fern does not produce plantlets, so can only be reproduced by means of its spores.

PLATYCERIUM VEITCHII (silver elkhorn). The greenish-white colour of the tiny matted hairs that cover the spore patches on the deep green fertile fronds give this fern its common name. The wide shield fronds are deeply and irregularly lobed, and quickly turn brown. The fertile fronds are stiff and most of them grow upwards. The spore patch is on the underside of the last section of the tapering eight-lobed fronds. It is a rare and beautiful plant in its natural habitat — the low rainfall areas of northern Queensland, Australia. The thick fleshy texture of the plant and the dense hairs help it to conserve moisture and withstand long periods without rain. Easily grown and hardy under cultivation, this species is also drought and frost resistant, but requires more light than the *Platycerium* species listed previously.

as they mature. The spores form in irregular patches covering all, or virtually all, of the tips. This species is hardy, often tolerating temperatures as low as –6°C (25°F). It is not difficult to cultivate. Old plants often form huge clumps that need strong support; trees may fall under the accumulated weight of an old plant.

PLATYCERIUM GRANDE. See *P. superbum*.

PLATYCERIUM HILLII (northern elkhorn). A native to northeast Australia, this fern is easily confused with *P. bifurcatum*. The top edge of the shield frond is almost uncut or has only shallow lobes. The spores form in irregular patches covering the underside of the last section of the lobes on the fertile fronds. This species is hardy and as easily cultivated as *P. bifurcatum*, but is not as frost resistant.

POLYPODIUM

Hare's Foot Ferns

This genus consists of a large and diverse group of ferns, most of which are distributed in the tropical and subtropical parts of the world. All species have a creeping rootstock. Most of the species in cultivation are epiphytes and are best grown in hanging baskets with good drainage, a light, open soil mix and in an airy situation. Because of the tropical and subtropical origins of most species, they are tender or semi-tender, and grow better indoors or in the glasshouse in cool temperate areas. They will tolerate minimum night temperatures of 15°C (60°F). They are also tolerant of medium to high light, bright diffused sunlight and a dry indoor atmosphere, but grow better with some humidity.

Australian species previously classified as part of the *Polypodium* genus are now classified under other genera including *Drynaria*, *Grammitis*, *Goniophlebium*, *Microsorium*, *Platycerium* and *Pyrrosia*.

POLYPODIUM ANGUSTIFOLIUM. An epiphyte with 30–40 cm (12–18 in) dark green and bronze fronds that are narrow and pointed. The creeping rhizome spreads just underneath the soil so that it is not evident. This species is best displayed in a hanging basket where it should be protected from dry and cold winds, direct sunlight and frost. It will tolerate strong light, but needs humidity.

POLYPODIUM AUREUM. See *Phlebodium aureum*.

POLYPODIUM AUSTRALE. See *P. vulgare*.

POLYPODIUM DRYOPTERIS. See *Gymnocarpium dryopteris*.

POLYPODIUM GONIOPHLEBIUM CV. KNIGHTIAE (knight's polypody). A large, deciduous fern which is semi-tender and very different from the species of which it is a cultivar. The species is a magnificent fern whose long, simply pinnate fronds give it a weeping character; the cultivar has compound feather-like pinnae. It is not difficult to grow and should be planted in a hanging basket to display it to best effect.

POLYPODIUM HERACLEUM. See *Aglaomorpha heraclea*.

POLYPODIUM INTEGRIFOLIUM CRISTATUM (crested climbing bird's nest fern). A native to Indonesia and tropical Asia, where it grows on trees rather like the *Asplenium nidus*. The complex fronds have ripples along the edges and irregular projections. The fronds grow to about 1 m (3 ft), becoming pendulous as their length and weight increase. This fern requires warmth and humidity at all times, but otherwise is easy to grow in the shade, if given regular watering.

POLYPODIUM INTERJECTUM. See *P. vulgare*.

POLYPODIUM PHEGOPTERIS. See *Thelypteris phegopteris*.

POLYPODIUM PHYLLITIDIS. Native to tropical America, this species resembles *Asplenium scolopendrium* (hart's-tongue fern). The smooth fronds grow in clumps from the underground rhizome and may be from 30–90 cm (12–36 in) in length, without a discernible stipe. It is hardy, though it does require some protection from frost, and grows well in the ground, in a hanging basket or in a pot. This fern should be kept moist and grown in shade with medium light.

POLYPODIUM SCANDENS. See *Microsorium scandens*.

POLYPODIUM SCOLOPENDRIUM. See *Phymatodes scolopendrium*.

POLYPODIUM SYLVATICUM. See *Drynaria quercifolia*.

POLYPODIUM VACCINIFOLIUM (alt. *Microgramma vaccinifolia*). This is a small creeping fern with white scales on the rhizome. It grows well in a hanging basket in a warm, humid atmosphere or in a terrarium. It is native to the subtropical regions of South America.

POLYPODIUM VULGARE (wart fern). This species is subject to much confusion — it is often referred to as *P. interjectum* and *P. australe*, and often the three

Polypodium vulgare

POLYSTICHUM

Shield Ferns

This is a large and widespread genus of generally hardy, tough, leathery ferns, given their common name because of the prominent shield-like indusia. They are small- to medium-growing ferns that form a cluster of filigreed fronds on top of an erect rhizome. Many cultivars and varieties are in cultivation.

POLYSTICHUM ACROSTICHOIDES (Christmas fern, dagger fern). A hardy, medium-sized species with glossy, dagger-shaped fronds in shades of blue-green, with stipes covered in rusty brown, harsh scales. The new fronds are covered in glistening white scales and are used by florists as ornamental foliage in the United States. This species is slow growing and shade tolerant.

POLYSTICHUM ACULEATUM (hard shield fern). This strong-growing hardy species is fairly common in Britain. The lower part of the stipe is densely clothed

species are considered to be quite distinct. It is a slow-growing, creeping fern which inhabits woodlands, stony ground and drystone walls in Britain, southern and southwestern Europe and southern Africa, and is also widespread in North America. This fern is easy to cultivate, but the soil must be well drained. The common name comes from the appearance of the indentations on the upper surface of the frond, which are formed by the deeply recessed sori on the underside.

POLYPODIUM VULGARE* VAR. *RAMOSUM (common polypody). A variety of *P. vulgare* found throughout Britain where it grows in hedge banks, mossy rocks and, sometimes as an epiphyte, in trees and on rock walls. The fronds branch repeatedly from the base, and are variable. It is a small-growing plant that is hardy and easy to cultivate, and attractive, if grown well. It requires a shady, damp area, but the ground should not be constantly wet.

Polystichum aculeatum

in large brown scales. One variety, the very hardy *P. aculeatum* var. *pulcherrimum gracillimum*, is an extremely beautiful fern; the fronds are very delicate with the hair-like pinnules ending in splayed tassels.

POLYSTICHUM POLYBLEPHARUM. See *P. setosum*.

POLYSTICHUM PROLIFERUM (mother shield fern). This is a hardy species native to Australia. As it ages, the rhizome forms a thick trunk covered in shiny brown scales which continue up the base of the stipe. It can be propagated from the many plantlets that form at the end of the fronds.

POLYSTICHUM SETIFERUM (soft shield fern). The rootstock of this fern is stout and often develops subsidiary crowns from buds on the frond bases. The crosiers are covered with glistening white scales which go brown as they mature. Considered hardy and easy to grow, this fern is tolerant of low light and should be kept moist. Many varieties of this species are in cultivation.

POLYSTICHUM SETOSUM (this is also known as *P. polyblepharum*). A semi-hardy species from Japan, which requires plenty of light and moist soil. The

fronds are deep green and lacy, and the crosiers appear to droop, giving them the appearance of a tassle and making the plant look as if it has dehydrated and needs watering.

POLYSTICHUM TSUS-SIMENSE (dwarf leather fern, Tsusima holly fern). A small, compact species from Japan and China with sharply cut, triangular fronds. It is hardy and is suited to growing in terrariums because of its small size. It is also suited to growing in a pot, or in a rock garden.

POLYSTICHUM VESTITUM (prickly shield fern). An easily grown shield fern that is native to New Zealand; and adaptable to most situations. This fern will not tolerate hot conditions.

PTERIDIUM

Brackens

The classification of these ferns is disputed among botanists. They are found throughout the world in a wide variety of habitats, but always where the soil is well drained. The brackens are well known for their ability to invade and render useless vast areas of pasture land by means of their slender, creeping, underground rhizomes. They are difficult to cultivate and transplant.

Bracken has been used as thatching for the roofs of buildings, packing for fresh market produce and an alternative to hay for bedding for farm animals. Although the crosiers are eaten in many countries, they are known to contain carcinogens.

PTERIDIUM AQUILINUM (common bracken in Britain and the Northern Hemisphere — also known as *Pteris aquilinum*). In Europe, cattle and horses are known to have been poisoned by this plant. The Australian plant *P. esculentum* is also poisonous.

Polystichum vestitum

Pteridium aquilinum

Pteris cretica cv. Rivertoniana

Some species of the *Pteridium* genus are cultivated. These include *P. aquilinum*, *P. crispum*, *P. cristatum*, *P. caudatum*, *P. latiusculum* (eastern bracken) and *P. pubescens* (western bracken).

PTERIDIUM ESCULENTUM (austral bracken, common bracken in Australia). This species is distributed widely throughout Australia, where it is always considered a nuisance. However, it is difficult to cultivate. The rhizomes are rich in starch and are used as a source of food in some countries; it is a staple of the diet of the indigenous people of the Canary Islands, New Zealand, the Society Islands and Australia. As previously mentioned, this plant is known to contain carcinogens and the reader should be wary of eating any of its parts.

PTERIS

Brakes

This is a large genus of ferns from the tropical and subtropical areas of the world. Most of the 250 or so species, and their many named cultivars and varieties, are greatly sought after. 'Pteris' comes from the Greek *pteron*, meaning feather, an allusion to the shape of the frond. The true species and the true varieties do not produce a great deal of variation in form or shape.

PTERIS AQUILINUM. See *Pteridium aquilinum*.

PTERIS ARGYRAEA. See *P. quadriaurita* var. *argyraea*.

PTERIS CRETICA (Cretan brake, ribbon brake). A fast-growing, small- to medium-sized fern. In its native Crete, it is found growing in the wild on shaded moist limestone walls where humidity is high and rainfall plentiful. It is semi-hardy, requires an open soil mix, and needs protection from extreme cold and strong light. Given these conditions, it is easy to cultivate. It will tolerate morning and late afternoon sunlight, and grows better in dry, exposed positions than do most ferns.

PTERIS CRETICA VAR. ALBO-LINEATA. Popular in Victorian times, this cultivar of *P. cretica* has a handsome broad band of creamy white on the centre of each wavy leaflet. Cultivation is similar to that of *P. cretica*, but this species should be kept out of direct sunlight.

PTERIS CRETICA CV. CHILDSII. A hybrid, clump-forming fern that is sterile and so can only be propagated by division. It requires protection from the cold and strong light. Cultivation is similar to that of *P. cretica*.

PTERIS CRETICA CV. PARKERI. A cultivar of *P. cretica* with broad, finely toothed leaflets. Cultivation is similar to that of *P. cretica*.

PTERIS CRETICA CV. RIVERTONIANA. A medium-sized variable fern with light green, feathery fronds like carrot tops. Variation occurs as crests on the pinnae. This species will tolerate strong light, but does best in partial shade. Cultivation is similar to that of *P. cretica*.

PTERIS CRETICA CV. WILSONII. A small popular cultivar produced in great numbers by commercial growers. It is an attractive fern with compact growth and bright green crested fronds. It should be planted in a protected position in the garden in acid, well-drained soil.

PTERIS CRETICA CV. WIMSETI-MULTICEPS (skeleton fern). An evergreen, creeping and variable cultivar. The common name comes from the skeletal, fragile appearance of the mature fronds. Cultivation is similar to that of *P. cretica*.

PTERIS DENTATA (toothed brake — also known as *P. flabellata*, *P. flaccida*). This species is a medium- to large-growing brake, similar to, but finer than, *P. tremula*. It requires moist conditions and is relatively easy to cultivate.

PTERIS ENSIFORMIS (slender brake). A compact, hardy species native to Australia, India, China, Japan, Malaysia and Polynesia where it grows in saline conditions on river foreshores and on the margins of forests. It has given rise to several cultivars with variegation in the foliage which are as easy to cultivate as the parent plant.

PTERIS ENSIFORMIS CV. EVERGEMIENSIS. A variegated and greatly sought after form of *P. ensiformis* (slender brake). This cultivar looks almost pure white, but on closer inspection, the dark green of the rest of the frond can be seen. It is a small-growing fern, slightly tender, which requires medium light and should be kept moist.

PTERIS ENSIFORMIS VAR. VICTORIAE (Victorian brake, queen's fern). A dimorphic, variegated fern that originally comes from India. It is sought after as a cultivated plant as it is small growing and ideal for a pot. Cultivation is the same as for the above cultivar.

PTERIS FLABELLATA. See *P. dentata*.

PTERIS FLACCIDA. See *P. dentata*.

PTERIS LONGIFOLIA. See *P. vittata*.

PTERIS MULTIFIDA (Chinese, spider or Huguenot fern — also known as *P. serrulata*). A small, hardy fern

Pteris multifida var. *angustata*

that has given rise to many crested forms and varieties including *P. multifida* cv. Cristata and *P. multifida* var. *angustata* (the latter is an adaptable plant). This species is easy to grow in the garden or in a pot; in the house or in the rock garden. The species and its cultivars and varieties should have extra calcium added to the soil.

PTERIS QUADRIAURITA VAR. ARGYRAEA (silver brake, striped brake — also known as *P. argyraea*). A large-growing fern with blue-green fronds banded with silver down the centre. This species is semi-tender and thus requires protection and should be kept moist. Another variegated form has red colouring in the fronds.

PTERIS SERRULATA. See *P. multifida*.

PTERIS TREMULA. A large, fast-growing fern native to Australia, New Zealand, Norfolk Island and Fiji, which is now cultivated throughout the world. It is easy to grow and makes a handsome pot plant; in the garden it propagates readily and will quickly occupy a large area. It will grow in a moderately sunny position with the soil on the dry side of moist. The crown sometimes rises above the soil, exposing the feeding roots and making them susceptible to dehydration; a mulch around the crown — not over it — will protect them.

Pteris quadriaurita var. *argyraea*

Pteris cretica cv. Childsii

PTERIS TRIPARTITA (giant brake in Australia, trisect brake in the United States). A very large, tender species of the *Pteris* genus which is easily grown in warm areas with medium light and moist conditions. The fronds can grow to 2.5 m (8 ft).

PTERIS VITTATA (Chinese brake, ladder brake, rusty brake — known commercially as *P. longifolia*). A widespread species found throughout tropical and temperate areas of Asia, Africa and Australia. It is a fast-growing, easily cultivated, medium-sized, dark green, graceful fern that will tolerate strong light. This species is intolerant of complete shade. It is hardy in slightly exposed and dry conditions.

PYROSSIA

Felt Ferns

This is a genus of about 100 epiphytic species from tropical rainforest areas of Africa, South America and southeast Australia. All species have simple fleshy fronds and are hardy and drought resistant despite their rainforest origins. They have minute hairs on their fronds which reduce their water loss. The species of this genus are suited to growing in rock gardens.

PYROSSIA LINGUA (tongue fern, Japanese felt fern). A small, slow-growing, creeping fern with thick, leathery fronds. It is semi-hardy to semi-tender and easily cultivated. This species is ideal for a pot and looks particularly attractive when encouraged to grow around the base of a hanging basket. There are a great many cultivars of this fern, one of which has a yellow variegation.

PYROSSIA RUPESTRIS (rock felt fern). A hardy, easily grown, dimorphic fern which is found in the open forests and rainforests of southeast Australia. The fronds will shrivel during times of drought, but recover with rain. It is an epiphyte that will thrive in a hanging basket and will also creep over rocks in the ground.

Pyrossia rupestris

Rumohra adiantiformis

RUMOHRA

Leather Ferns

This genus consists of medium-sized terrestrial or epiphytic ferns native to the tropics south of the equator. Some are lithophytic, growing on rocks and cliff faces.

RUMOHRA ADIANTIFORMIS (leather fern in the United States, leathery shield fern or shield hare's foot in Australia). The common name comes from the coarse appearance of the fronds. They are frequently used by florists in arrangements because they last for several weeks when cut and placed in water. Despite the coarse fronds, it is a handsome durable plant for the house or for the garden. In the garden, because of its creeping habit it will cover a large area. In conditions of high humidity, it will also climb trees. This is its habit in New Zealand, where it is often confused with some members of the *Davallia* and *Polystichum* genera. It is semi-hardy to semi-tender, requiring medium light conditions and moist to dry soil. Tolerant of morning and late afternoon sunlight, this fern does well in slightly dry and exposed positions.

STENOCHLAENA

Climbing Ferns

This is a genus of dimorphic, climbing ferns from the rainforests of Malaysia and Africa; one species is found in Australia.

STENOCHLAENA PALUSTRIS (climbing swamp fern). This Australian species is easy to propagate and to grow. It requires shade but plenty of light. This fern is an epiphyte, despite its natural swamp habitat. For this reason, it should be kept very moist but well drained at the same time. If properly managed, its rampant growth — unusual in the fern world — makes it very rewarding to grow. It is a useful, but unusual, plant with which to cover a shaded pergola. It is tender and needs protection from frost. The old fronds are shiny with finely serrated margins and new fronds are copper coloured.

STICHERUS

Fan Ferns, Umbrella Ferns

This is a genus of bushy ferns with umbrella-like fronds which is not cultivated widely outside Australia and New Zealand.

STICHERUS FLABELLATUS (shiny fan fern, umbrella fern). A very slow-growing, but robust fern, which branches in umbrella-like fashion in one to four tiers. In its natural habitat, in eastern Australia, Papua New Guinea and New Zealand, it lies in great tangled masses like soft mists on top of low-growing shrubs. It makes an attractive plant for a large pot in a moist garden position, but it should be grown from small plants as large specimens will often not recover from disturbance.

STICHERUS TENER (silky fan fern). Very similar to *S. flabellatus* in habit, growth and cultivation. Its fronds are a shiny light green with entire pinnules (*S. flabellatus* has serrated pinnules).

Stenochlaena palustris

Sticherus flabellatus

TECTARIA

This is a genus of approximately 200 medium- to large-growing ferns with coarse pale green fronds. The species grow naturally in tropical and subtropical parts of the world.

TECTARIA GEMMIFERA (button fern in the United States, snail fern in Australia — also known commercially as *T. cicutaria*). The common name comes from the masses of buds which form on the fronds. New plants may be easily propagated from the buds which are well developed by the time they are shed from the mother plant (each bud already has several well-developed crosiers and a scaly exterior to protect it from dehydration). It is a medium-sized fern that is semi-tender due to its tropical origins. It needs medium light and to be kept moist.

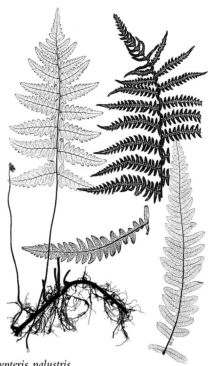

Thelypteris palustris

THELYPTERIS

Wood Ferns, Hay Ferns

This is a worldwide genus of about 800 species of, mostly, medium-sized ferns with narrow fronds borne in clusters along a creeping rhizome.

THELYPTERIS HEXAGONOPTERA (southern beech fern in the United States, broad beech fern in Britain). One of the two beech ferns found growing in North America — *T. phegopteris* (northern beech fern) is the other — this species is the largest and most erect, and grows naturally in sunny, open positions. It is considered hardy, but is deciduous in cold conditions.

THELYPTERIS NOVEBORACENIS (New York fern). A delicate and elegant looking fern from North America which spreads rapidly where it grows

naturally on the edges of marshes and in moist sunny clearings in woodlands. The fronds appear to grow in tufts of three or four together, along a creeping rootstock. It is hardy, but deciduous, and tolerates strong light. This fern should be kept moist.

THELYPTERIS PALUSTRIS (marsh fern — also known as *Dryopteris thelypteris*). This species is a dainty-looking, but vigorous, invasive fern growing up to 1.5 m (5 ft) high. It is native to central Europe, India, China, Japan and central North America, where it grows naturally in marshes and on the edges of streams. This fern can be invasive in the garden. Lime should be added to its soil and it should be planted in a large pot.

THELYPTERIS PHEGOPTERIS (beech fern in Britain — also known as *Polypodium phegopteris, Dryopteris phegopteris*). This is a slow-growing, hardy and deciduous species native to Europe, Asia and North America. It prefers shade and acid soil, with the addition of leaf mould.

TODEA

King Ferns

This is a genus consisting of two species of large terrestrial ferns which, as they get older, form fibrous trunks. Several crowns of fronds may grow from the trunks. These ferns are found growing in eastern Australia, New Zealand, Papua New Guinea and South Africa.

TODEA BARBARA. This is a semi-hardy and adaptable fern that becomes tree-like and very handsome with age. The caudex may reach 1–1.5 m (4–5 ft) in height and 1 m (3 ft) in diameter. Multiple crowns may develop on the caudex, enabling the plant to grow to massive proportions for a fern. It will grow in an exposed situation, under which conditions the fronds broaden and shorten. It will also grow in the shade, where the fronds become elongated. Because of this adaptability, the king fern makes an excellent potted plant for both in and out of doors. It should be given plenty of room to grow so that its fronds can spread. The spores have a very brief lifespan, and they therefore need to be sown while they are still fresh.

WOODSIA

This is a genus of small alpine and woodland ferns found in North America, China, Japan, Korea and Europe. Only a few of the rather rare species are cultivated.

WOODSIA OBTUSA (blunt-lobed woodsia). This is a small and very hardy species that is easy to grow. It is found growing naturally among limestone rocks in Britain and North America. Given its natural habitat, it is especially suited to cultivation in rock gardens or in small pots.

WOODWARDIA

Chain Ferns

This is a genus of medium- to large-growing, easily cultivated terrestrial ferns of coarse texture which are native to North America, Europe, Asia and the Philippines. The common name comes from the appearance of the sori, which are arranged in two precise rows on both sides of the midrib of each frond. They are strong-growing woodland plants which thrive in moist, acid soil and will tolerate a little sunlight.

WOODWARDIA RADICANS (European chain fern). A hardy, strong-growing and easily cultivated fern from North America, southern Europe, Asia and the Atlantic Islands. The fronds, sometimes 2 m (6 ft) long, produce plantlets near to, or at, their tips. The plantlets grow quite large while still attached to the frond. This fern needs plenty of space so that the elegant arching shape of its fronds can be appreciated. New fronds are pink; the older fronds, pale green. During the winter months, mature fronds take on a purple tint, making it one of the most colourful species of the fern family. It is hardy, fast growing and tolerant of strong light; but it should be kept moist at all times.

Woodwardia radicans

TREE FERNS

Tree ferns are the diminutive descendants of the great ferns which, along with the giant mosses and horsetails, made up most of the world's vegetation in the Carboniferous period. The first of the vascular plants and hundreds of millions of years older than the seed-bearing plants, their remains make up the coal seams that are to be found in warm temperate areas of the world today.

Tree ferns grow mostly in tropical and warm temperate zones of the world. Only a few, which grow in the *Nothofagus* (southern beech) forests of Victoria and Tasmania in Australia and the *Metrosideros* (rata) woods of New Zealand, will tolerate frost and prolonged cold. A tree fern with snow weighing down its fronds is a beautiful but unusual sight.

Most ferns that form a trunk and carry their fronds in a whorl at the top are referred to as 'tree ferns'. Ferns with such growth habits are found in several genera including *Sadleria*, *Blechnum*, *Ctenitis*, *Cyathea*, *Dicksonia*, *Todea* and *Cibotium*. Under the tree fern heading in this book, only the commonly cultivated genera *Cibotium*, *Ctenitis*, *Cyathea* and *Dicksonia* are listed. Other cultivated ferns with a tree-like habit are *Blechnum gibbum*, *Blechnum brasiliense* and *Todea barbara*. These are listed individually in the main fern list.

Recently there has been a great deal of confusion over the classification of tree ferns into appropriate genera. Some books list the commonly cultivated tree ferns under the genera *Sphaeropteris* and *Alsophila*; this book lists them under *Cyathea* and *Dicksonia* as these are names that are probably more familiar to most gardeners and have, so far, the longest standing. The genera *Cyathea* and *Dicksonia* have between them about 700 species, but only a quite small portion of these (about 150 species) is cultivated.

CIBOTIUM

This is a genus of about ten large-growing tree ferns from Asia, Hawaii and Central America.

Cibotium chamissoi

CIBOTIUM CHAMISSOI (man fern). This is a beautiful, strong-growing tree fern which may reach huge proportions in its native habitat in Hawaii. The upper portion of the trunk and the lower portions of the stipes are covered by silky, golden-brown hairs. It is a difficult fern to grow, but is included in this list because it is mentioned earlier as the fern used in a short-lived and unsuccessful 19th-century business venture, which involved marketing the hair-like growth on the stipes for use as a filling for pillows (see pp. 25–26).

CIBOTIUM GLAUCUM (hapu, Hawaiian tree fern). A large semi-tender species the fronds of which are carried high and tend to arch more gracefully than those of the *Cyathea* and *Dicksonia* species. The leaf bases and trunks are covered with tan silky hairs. It is not widely cultivated outside the warm areas of the west coast of the United States of America. It requires warmth, plenty of light and moist, humid conditions.

CIBOTIUM SCHIEDEI (Mexican tree fern). The gracefully arching fronds, the caudex covered with lustrous yellow-brown hairs, and the white bloom on the undersides of the pale green fronds make this one of the most handsome of all the species of the *Cibotium* genus. It grows slowly, and because of this, makes an ideal tub plant. In its natural habitat it grows to about 4.5 m (15 ft). It needs glasshouse conditions to grow well outside warm temperate areas.

CTENITIS

This is a genus of medium- to large-growing ferns from pantropic areas of Central and South America and the West Indies. Individual species are grown mostly by fern collectors.

CTENITIS SLOANEI (American tree fern, Florida tree fern). This is a large, tender species that is sometimes cultivated on the west coast of the United States of America.

CYATHEA

This is a complex genus of about 800 species distributed widely throughout the warm temperate and tropical areas of the world. Generally the cultivated species listed here are hardy and vigorous plants that are suitable for pot cultivation while they are young and still relatively small. They need some protection from frost while young, but if fronds *are* damaged, the plants recover quickly. They are easily propagated by spores. Species of this genus, other than *C. australis*, may be transplanted from the crown and upper part of the caudex without roots.

CYATHEA AUSTRALIS (rough tree fern). This is the common large tree fern found in the southeast of Australia and is distinguishable by the short, sharp, rasp-like protuberances and masses of shiny brown scales on the stipe base and upper trunk. *C. australis* grows up to 12 m (40 ft) tall with a frond spread of

Cyathea dealbata

about 9 m (30 ft). This fern must be transplanted with its roots intact. Unscrupulous fern dealers remove these native ferns from their natural habitat, slashing them through with a chain saw and selling them to the unsuspecting public. The ferns continue to grow while embryonic fronds are still present, but without roots they do not produce new fronds and the plant dies. If planted with its roots intact, the rough tree fern is easily grown. It is a hardy plant tolerating full sun if well watered.

CYATHEA BAILEYANA (wig tree fern). This fern has a wig-like growth at the top of the trunk that is bright green when young and reddish-brown when it matures. It grows to 5 m (17 ft) with a spread of 6 m (20 ft) and is frost tender.

CYATHEA COOPERI (Australian tree fern). This species has a trunk patterned with the scars left by the fallen fronds. Its unfurling crosiers are covered with long, silky white scales. This is a fast-growing and hardy species reaching a height of about 12 m (40 ft) with a spread of 12 m (40 ft).

CYATHEA COOPERI VAR. ROBUSTA and **CYATHEA COOPERI VAR. BRENTWOOD**. These are variants of the species which have been named in the United States. The colouring of the fronds is the most distinguishing feature of this species. The fronds of var. *robusta* are darker than those of the parent species; those of var. *brentwood* are a lighter green. The stipes of the species are pale green (those on var. *brentwood* have yellowish-green stipes and those on var. *robusta* are almost black). The trunks of the three ferns are also distinct. The species has the smallest trunk, var. *robusta*'s is slightly larger and var. *brentwood*'s is considerably larger. Both variants are suitable container plants and thrive out of doors in warm temperate areas.

CYATHEA DEALBATA (ponga, silver king fern). The fronds of this hardy tree fern are New Zealand's

Cyathea woollsiana

national emblem. They are silver underneath giving the plant its common name, but they are not robust and need protection from the wind or they become very untidy. This species grows to 9 m (30 ft).

CYATHEA MEDULLARIS (korau, mamaku, black tree fern). A species that is native to New Zealand and Polynesia and grows to 7.5 m (25 ft).

CYATHEA VIEILLARDII. This is a slender, spreading tree fern from New Caledonia. It is easily grown in a constantly warm situation, in shade or in partial sunlight.

CYATHEA WOOLLSIANA. This is an attractive slender tree fern with broad arching fronds which is found in the mountain areas of Queensland, Australia. It is hardy but grows best in the shade and is slightly frost tender. At maturity it can reach about 5 m (16 ft) with a frond span of 9 m (30 ft). It makes an excellent tub plant.

DICKSONIA

This is a commonly cultivated, but relatively small genus of approximately 25 species distributed widely throughout the world. They are considered rather primitive. The most graceful and hardy of the plants that are rather loosely called 'tree ferns', they are not trees in any sense of the world. Other species of tree ferns form 'trunks'; the 'trunk' of the *Dicksonia* genus, despite a height of sometimes 4.5 m (15 ft), consists entirely of a cluster of dead roots and dead frond bases. These ferns are really epiphytes growing on the top of an entwined, elongated mass of their own dead matter. The young roots must make their way down through this accumulation of dead matter to find nourishment. In the wild, the trunk is usually covered with epiphyte plants which trap humus and moisture for the roots as they grow down to the ground. The plants do not thrive unless the so-called trunk, or root system, is protected and kept moist — this is often an unsuspected cause of failure in cultivation. In their natural habitat, when large specimens of this species fall and lie supported horizontally by other trees, their roots continue to grow vertically, eventually forming a dense, curtain-like mass.

These ferns should be planted where their arching fronds are displayed to advantage and in a situation where there is sufficient protection to keep the growth soft and bright green. At least one-third of the trunk should be planted in the ground so that the roots descending from the crown are able to quickly reach nourishment, and so that the plant is not continually rocked by wind and the roots dislodged. The trunk should be kept damp and the crown given some overhead protection for a few months. All species are easily raised from spores.

DICKSONIA ANTARCTICA (soft tree fern). A hardy native plant of the eastern states of Australia, including Tasmania, and a widely cultivated fern. The specimens growing in the northern extremities of the natural habitats are less robust and also less common than those which grow in Victoria and Tasmania. This is the tree fern that is sold in thousands by nurseries.

D. antarctica may grow to 15 m (48 ft) tall with a frond span of 9 m (30 ft); up to 40 fronds may unfurl at a time, making a spectacular sight. It is an ideal potted plant which will grow for many years in the same large pot. It requires little space for its roots, and thrives on regular feeding with leaf mould and bone meal. Pots should be well insulated or mulched as this fern must have plenty of water. This is the tree fern that is seen growing at the snow line. It is easily propagated from its spores.

DICKSONIA FIBROSA (wheki-ponga). A slow-growing New Zealand species closely allied to *D. antarctica*, but much less prickly, and smaller, growing to only

Dicksonia youngiae

Dicksonia antarctica

2–6 m (6–20 ft). It is a hardy fern and grows well in conditions similar to those of the Australian species; but is not a strong-growing plant. Its true trunk is only 8–10 cm (3–4 in) in diameter, but when covered with a mass of fibrous aerial roots it looks a great deal thicker.

DICKSONIA SQUARROSA (rough dicksonia, wheki). A native of New Zealand, this species has a trunk reaching to 6 m (20 ft) and a crown of stiff, leathery, dark green fronds up to 2.5 m (8 ft) long. The trunk sometimes develops secondary growth below ground which produces runners and new growth if the main

trunk is damaged. In the wild, these runners form thickets of young ferns. An example of this growth is seen in the Ballarat Gardens in Victoria, Australia, where this fern has spread through the old fernery.

DICKSONIA YOUNGIAE (bristly tree fern). A hardy, fast-growing and attractive fern; the upper trunk and stipes are covered with stiff, reddish-brown bristles. It comes from rainforests in northern New South Wales and Queensland in Australia; but is rather rare. Offsets which form on the trunk can be removed with a sharp knife and potted, but they are slow to establish.

FILMY FERNS

The filmy ferns are thought to be amongst the most primitive of living plants and form a quite distinctive, yet homogeneous, group within the fern family.

Their fronds are the dimension of only one cell in depth, giving them their dainty, almost translucent, appearance and making them totally dependent on extremely high humidity in their immediate atmosphere. Their dependence on water vapour suggests that they were one of the first vascular plants.

The fragile structure of their fronds enables them to absorb moisture readily in a liquid or vapour form from the atmosphere; but they can also lose moisture readily so that they quickly become a dehydrated shrivelled mass if they are without it for too long.

Botanists regard the filmy ferns as curiosities because the way in which they carry their large spore cases on the ends of veins, at the margins of fronds, is distinct and less complicated than that of other ferns.

The filmy ferns are difficult to cultivate in the open garden and most glasshouse conditions are too arid for them. They can be cultivated if a part of the glasshouse is adapted to their needs with walls lined with spaghnum moss kept moist by trickling water, a misting device or by means of a humidifier (so that humidity is almost 100%). Individual plants may be grown directly on the moss or in pots buried in the moss. They will grow well under these conditions provided that temperatures are moderate and light is kept low.

The commonly cultivated genera include *Hymenophyllum*, *Mecodium* and *Trichomanes*. They are ideal plants for a terrarium where the atmosphere can be maintained at almost dewpoint, but they should not be cultivated in the terrarium with other plants as their roots form a dense mass that may overwhelm such plants.

Trichomanes radicans

Trichomanes angustatum

AQUATIC FERNS

The two most frequently cultivated aquatic fern genera, Azolla and Marsilea, are often dismissed as fern 'oddities' because of their very unfern-like appearance, but they are true ferns in their structure and reproductive methods.

Ceratopteris is another genus of cultivated aquatic ferns. It is much more like the accepted form of a fern.

The leaves of the *Azolla* have two lobes, the lower of which contains a nitrogen-fixing alga; in parts of Asia this is used to advantage by rice growers and the fern is planted as a green manure crop before rice is sown.

AZOLLA

Mosquito Ferns, Water Ferns, Carolina Pond Ferns

This is a small genus of floating aquatic ferns (sometimes referred to as the mosquito fern) which spread rapidly over large areas of still or gently moving water by means of self-division. There are six or so species, which are widely spread through-out the world.

Despite tiny leaves and a dainty appearance, the species are surprisingly hardy and will grow strongly, so much so that they will frequently overwhelm other aquatic plants. The *Azolla* genus will re-establish quickly even if it is removed in handfuls from ornamental ponds. During certain times of the year, the fronds take on a distinct rusty red hue.

All species live in a symbiotic relationship with a blue-green alga called *Anabaena azolla*, which lives in pouches on the ferns' leaves. All species grow easily in pools and ponds in sunlight or shade.

CERATOPTERIS

Two species of dimorphic ferns from Southeast Asia, Central and South America and the West Indies.

CERATOPTERIS PTEROIDES. Similar to *C. thalictroides*. This fern can be cultivated in a tropical fish aquarium.

CERATOPTERIS THALICTROIDES (water fern). A fragile, light green fern that grows in mud or completely submerged in water. When mature, the fertile fronds float away from the parent to form new plants. It is easily grown in ponds in warm temperate areas and, with protection, in cool temperate areas. The plant is well suited to an aquarium and is edible.

MARSILEA

Nardoos, Water Shamrocks, Water Cloves, Pepperworts

This is a genus of about 60 species of aquatic ferns which look like floating four-leaved clover plants, covered with silky hairs. Their method of reproduction is highly developed for a member of the fern family, and is very close to that of flowering plants. The spores form in cases called sporocarps, carried at the bottom of the short stipes. Two different spores are produced — megaspores, which germinate into prothalli-bearing archegonia, or female reproductive organs; and microspores, which germinate into prothalli bearing antheridia, or male reproductive organs.

The nardoos are easily grown in sheltered boggy places on the edges of ponds or in wide, shallow pots with the soil kept constantly moist.

FERN ALLIES AND MASQUERADERS

Fern allies make up a very ancient group of plants which developed and reached their peak during the Carboniferous period. They are commonly known as horsetails (Class Sphenopsida), club mosses (Class Lycopodida, which are the most primitive of the classes of fern allies), quillworts and whisk ferns (Class Psiloptopsida).

Like true ferns, the fern allies reproduce by means of spores, but unlike true ferns they do not produce a true frond, but a much simpler and smaller leaf borne on flattened branches. Another important difference is that the fern allies carry their spores in cases between the leaves and crowded into club-like cones (called 'strobili').

The most commonly cultivated fern allies are the genera *Lycopodium* and *Selaginella*; both belong to the Class Lycopida, and are closely related.

The *Selaginella* species, commonly called club mosses, make up a large genus of about 600 species found throughout the world. They are generally small plants of soft, mossy or fern-like appearance that are hardy and tolerant of low light, although humidity should be kept high in order to maintain an attractive appearance. Their low-growing habit makes them useful as a ground cover in cool, damp places. They make attractive individual potted plants and combine well with tall arching ferns in a hanging basket. Humidity must be adequate and soil kept moist for these plants to thrive.

The tassel ferns make up a distinct group within the *Lycopodium* genus. They are epiphytes which have long pendulous stems bearing crowded scale-like leaves with tassels on their tips. They make ideal plants for hanging baskets, but because of their tropical origins must be in a protected position even in warm areas and given glasshouse protection in less temperate areas. The fronds are delicate and need protection from the sun and wind.

Many plants imitate the fern, but none so successfully as some members of the *Asparagus* genus — a genus of about 100 species belonging to the lily family. They come from South Africa and were first collected at the end of the 19th century.

A. plumosa, the species with the soft feathery fronds, is most often mistaken for a fern. It will climb, in a scrambling manner, in a sheltered place in the garden. *A. sprengerii* is the bushy plant, the fronds of which elongate in low light conditions. Both these *Asparagus* species are hardy plants, tolerating low temperatures and shady positions. They prefer a confined root space and should never be allowed to dry out. Unlike ferns, they are prickly to the touch.

Selaginella

Asparagus plumosa

GLOSSARY

ANTHERIDIUM The part of the prothallus that contains the sperm-producing male sexual organs. Plural *antheridia*.

APOGAMY The production of a sporophyte from the tissues of the prothallus without the normal fertilisation process.

APOSPORY The production of a prothallus on the tissues of a sporophyte without the normal process of fertilisation.

ARCHEGONIUM The part of the prothallus containing the egg-producing female sexual organ. Plural *archegonia*.

BULBIL A small bulb-like bud which is borne on a frond and develops into a plantlet.

CAUDEX The trunk of a tree fern. Also, though not often used, any small erect fern rhizome.

CIRCINATE VERNATION A typical fern's method of growing, i.e. crosier uncurls upwards gradually; if a leaf is compound, the main axis uncoils upwards and lateral parts outwards.

CROSIER An uncoiled young frond.

CULTIVAR A plant variety developed under cultivation.

DIMORPHIC Bearing two types of fronds, usually one fertile and the other sterile.

EPIPHYTE A plant which grows on another for support — not a parasite.

FALSE INDUSIUM A spore case covering formed by a reflexed leaf margin.

FERN ALLIES Relatives of ferns which reproduce by means of spores, but which have a much simpler tissue structure.

FERTILE In relation to fronds, refers to those which carry spores.

FORM A botanical division below a species. Plural *forma*.

FRIABLE Soil which is loose in texture.

FROND The part of a fern called a leaf in other plants.

GAMETOPHYTE A small, flat plant bearing the reproductive organs, i.e. the prothallus.

GENUS A botanical and zoological division which groups related species. Plural *genera*.

GLAUCOUS A blue-grey colour.

HYBRID A plant resulting from the crossing of two plants of different characteristics.

INDUSIUM — The membrane covering the sorus or cluster of spore cases.

LITHOPHYTE — A plant that grows on rocks.

MUTATION — A sudden change in plants and animals due to changes in the genes or chromosomes. These genetic changes may be inherited by future generations.

PINNA — The primary segment of the divided frond. Plural *pinnae*.

PINNULE — The secondary pinna.

PROLIFEROUS — The vegetative rather than the sexual (reproduction).

PROTHALLUS — The tiny, flat plant which grows from a spore and carries the reproductive organs. Plural *prothalli*.

PUPS — The common name given to new plants which form on species of the *Platycerium* genus.

RACHIS — The midrib of a frond.

RHIZOME — The stem which produces roots and grows horizontally above or below ground, or grows vertically, e.g. climbing ferns and tree ferns.

ROOTSTOCK — The part of the stem which is underground and to which the roots are attached.

SCALES — Small, flat, papery structures borne on stems and rhizomes.

SORUS — A cluster of spore cases. Plural *sori*.

SPORANGIUM — The capsule containing the spores. Plural *sporangia*.

SPORE — The dust-like cell which becomes the prothallus.

SPORELING — A young fern which has developed from a prothallus.

SPOROPHYTE — The asexual fern generation or spore-bearing plant.

STIPE — The stalk of the frond from the rhizome to the leaf blade.

STOLON — A stem capable of producing a new plant at its tip.

STRAIGHT VERNATION — The arrangement of new fronds that push through the soil in a bent form and then uncoil laterally.

SYNONYM — An alternate, though not necessarily correct, scientific name.

TERRESTRIAL — A botanical term describing a plant that grows on the ground.

VARIETY — A botanical division below a species, but above a form.

VERNATION — The arrangement of unexpanded leaves or fronds in a bud.

XEROPHYTE — A plant adapted to dry conditions.

ZYGOTE — The fertilised egg.

FERN SOCIETIES

AUSTRALIA

Fern Society of South Australia
PO Box 711
GPO
Adelaide SA 5001

Fern Society of Victoria
PO Box 45
Heidelberg Vic 3081

Fern Society of Western Australia
C/o Mrs G. E. J. Bromley
73 Point Walter Road
Bicton WA 6157

Fern Study Group of the Society for
    Growing Australian Plants
C/o M. Woolett
3 Currawong Place
Como West NSW 2226

Sunshine Coast Fern Society
PO Box 47
Woombye Qld 4559

Tasmanian Fern Society
C/o Julie Haas
72 Bush Creek Road
Lenah Valley Tas 7008

CHINA

Fern Society of China
C/o Prof. K. H. Shing
Institute of Botany
Academia Sinica
Beijing 100044

INDIA

Indian Fern Society
C/o Prof. S. S. Bir
Department of Botany
Punjab University
Patiala 147002

JAPAN

Japanese Pteridological Society
Botanical Gardens
University of Tokyo
Hakusan 3-7-1
Bunkyo-Ku
Tokyo 112

Nippon Fernist Club
C/o Institute of Forest Botany
Faculty of Agriculture
University of Tokyo
Hongo
Bunkyo-Ku
Tokyo 113

THE NETHERLANDS

Nederlandse Varemvelemiging
C/o J. J. Comijs
2 Aalroslaan 12
6881 R H Velp

NEW ZEALAND

Nelson Fern Society Inc. of New Zealand
C/o Mrs J. Bonnington
9 Bay View Road
Atawhai
Nelson

Waikato Fern Club
C/o Mrs E. McKenzie
164 Upper Dinsdale Road
Hamilton

THE PHILIPPINES

Fern Society of the Philippines
National Museum
P. Burgos Street
Manila

SWITZERLAND

Schweizerische Vereiningung der Farnfreunde
C/o Dr. J. J. Schneller
Institüt Für Systematische Botanik
Zollikerstrasse 107
CH-8008 Zurich

UNITED KINGDOM

British Pteridological Society
C/o Miss A. M. Paul
Department of Botany
The Natural History Museum
Cromwell Road
London SW7 5BD

UNITED STATES OF AMERICA

American Fern Society
C/o Dr W. C. Taylor
Botany Department
Milwaukee Public Museum
800 W. Wells Street
Milwaukee WI 53233

Birmingham Fern Society
C/o Mrs R. E. Smith
4736 7th Avenue South
Birmingham AL 35222

Corpus Christi Fern Society
C/o P. Coleman
438 Claremont Street
Corpus Christi TX 78412

Delaware Valley Fern Society
C/o Mrs M. B. Peterson
22 West Southampton Avenue
Philadelphia PA 19118

Fern Study Group of the Northwest
    Horticultural Society
C/o Mr N. Hall
1230 North East 88th Street
Seattle WA 98115

Los Angeles International Tropical
    Fern Society
PO Box 90943
Pasadena CA 90638
OR C/o 14895 Gardenhill Drive
La Mirada CA 90638

Louisiana Fern Society
C/o F. H. Yeargers
901 Robert E. Lee Boulevard
New Orleans LA 70124

Memphis Fern Society
C/o Ms B. Feuerstein
2357 Thornwood Lane
Memphis TN 38138

BIBLIOGRAPHY

Allen, D. E. (1969), *The Victorian Fern Craze: A History of Pteridomania*, Hutchinson and Co. Ltd, London.

Bailey, F. M. (1881), *The Fern World of Australia*, Gordon & Gotch, Brisbane.

Birkenhead, J. (no date), *Ferns and Fern Culture*, H. B. May and Sons, London.

Bower, F. O. (1923), *The Ferns*, Cambridge University Press, Cambridge, vol. I 1923, vol. II 1926, vol. III 1928.

Chinnock, R. J. & E. Heath (1981), *Common Ferns and Fern Allies*, Mobil New Zealand Nature Series, A. H. & A. W. Reed Ltd, Christchurch.

Crittenden, M. (1978), *The Fern Book*, Celestial Arts, Millbrae, California.

Crookes, M. (1963), *New Zealand Ferns*, 6th ed., Whitcombe & Tombs, Christchurch.

Dobbie, H. B. & M. Crookes (1951), *New Zealand Ferns*, Whitcombe & Tombs Ltd, Auckland.

Druery, C. T. (1910), *British Ferns and Their Varieties*, G. Routledge & Sons, London.

Elliot, W. R. & D. L. Jones (1982), *Encyclopaedia of Australian Plants Suitable for Cultivation*, Lothian Publishing Co. Pty Ltd, Melbourne, vol. 2, no. 1, pp. 157–9.

Fisher, M. E. & L. Ward (1976), *New Zealand Ferns in Your Garden*, William Collins (NZ) Ltd, Auckland.

Foster, F. G. (1976), *Ferns to Know and Grow*, Hawthorn Books, New York.

Goudey, C. J. (1985), '*Maidenhair Ferns in Cultivation*', Lothian Publishing Co., Melbourne.

Grounds, R. (1974), *Ferns*, Pelham Books, London.

Guilcher, J. M. & R. H. Noailles (1973), *A Fern is Born*, Sterling Publishing Co., New York.

Heath, E. & R. J. Chinnock (1974), *Ferns and Fern Allies of New Zealand*, A. H. & A. W. Reed Pty Ltd, Wellington.

Hibberd, S. (1879), *The Fern Garden*, Groombridge & Sons, London.

Hooker, Sir W. J. (1862), *Garden Ferns*, Lovell Reeve & Co., London.

Hoshizaki, B. J. (1970), 'The Genus *Adiantum* in Cultivation', *Baileya*, vol. 17, pp. 97–191.

Hoshizaki, B. J. (1979), *Fern Growers Manual*, Alfred A. Knopf, New York.

Hoshizaki, B. J. (1981), 'The Fern Genus *Davallia* in Cultivation (Davalliaceae)', *Baileya*, vol. 21, pp. 1–42.

Hoshizaki, B. J. (1981), 'The Genus *Pyrrosia* in Cultivation', *Baileya*, vol. 21, pp. 43–50.

Jones, D. L. & S. C. Clemesha (1981), *Australian Ferns and Fern Allies*, A. H. & A. W. Reed Pty Ltd, Sydney.

Jones, D. L. & C. J. Goudey (1981), *Exotic Ferns in Australia*, A. H. & A. W. Reed Pty Ltd, Sydney.

Jones, D. L. & C. J. Goudey (1984), *Ferns in Australia*, A. H. & A. W. Reed Pty Ltd, Sydney.

Kaye, R. (1968), *Hardy Ferns*, Faber & Faber Ltd, London.

Kaye, R. (1980), 'Ferns', *Wisley Handbook*, 32, Royal Horticultural Society, London.

Macself, A. J. (1952), *Ferns for Garden and Greenhouse*, W. H. & L. Collingridge Ltd, London.

Olson, W. W. (1977), *The Fern Dictionary*, Los Angeles Fern Society, Los Angeles.

Rogers, P. (1986), *Safer Pest Control for Australian Homes & Gardens*, Kangaroo Press, NSW.

Rush, R. (1984), *A Guide to Hardy Ferns*, British Pteridological Society, London.

Shaver, J. M. (1954), *Ferns of the Eastern Central States*, Dover Publications, New York.

Smith, J. (1875), *Historia Filicum*, Macmillan, London.

Smith J. (1879), *Ferns British and Foreign*, David Bogue, London.

Step, E. (1908), *Wayside and Woodland Ferns*, Frederick Warne & Co., London.

Sim, T. R. (1915), *The Ferns of South Africa*, Cambridge.

Small, J. K. (1918), *Ferns of Tropical Florida*, Published by Author, New York.

Small, J. K. (1975), *Ferns of the Vicinity of New York*, Dover Publications, New York.

Taylor, T. M. C. (1970), *Pacific Northwest Ferns and Their Allies*, University Press, Toronto.

Thieret, J. W. (1980), *Louisiana Ferns and Fern Allies*, Lafayette Natural History Museum, Louisiana.

Tryon, R. M. & A. F. Tryon (1982), *Ferns and Allied Plants with Special Reference to Tropical America*, Springer-Verlag, New York.

Wakefield, N. A. (1975), *The Ferns of Victoria & Tasmania*, revised by J. H. Willis, Field Naturalists' Club of Victoria, Melbourne.

Wherry, E. T. (1964), *The Southern Fern Guide*, American Fern Society, New York.

Wiley, F. A. (1973), *Ferns of the Northeastern United States*, Dover Publications Inc., New York.

Willis, J. C. (1973), *A Dictionary of Flowering Plants and Ferns*, 8th ed., revised by H. K. Airy Shaw, Cambridge University Press, Cambridge.

INDEX

Page references in bold type refer to illustrations.

PICTURE CREDITS

PHOTOGRAPHS

Photographs are in page order l (left); r (right); t (top); b (bottom).
Unless otherwise stated, all photographs © Gillean Dunk. In all other cases, copyright remains with
individual photographers or institutions.

Front cover, Ivy Hansen; p. i, Ivy Hansen; pp. iv–v, John Squire; p. 1, from *The Greening of Gondwana* (Mary E. White), photo Jim Frazier; p. 4, from *The Greening of Gondwana* (Mary E. White), photo Jim Frazier; p. 5, George Greblo; p. 17, *Home Beautiful*, photo Gary Chowanetz; p. 21, Bay Picture Library; pp. 32–33, Ivy Hansen; p. 36, John Squire; p. 53, Bay Picture Library; pp. 56–57, Ivy Hansen; p. 60, The Photo Library, Sydney; p. 61, John Squire; pp. 64–65, Ivy Hansen; p. 68, Bay Picture Library; p. 69, Bay Picture Library; p. 71, Bay Picture Library; p. 72, Bay Picture Library; p. 73, Bay Picture Library; pp. 76–77, Ivy Hansen; p. 81, Sporting Pix; p. 88, Ivy Hansen; p. 89, Ivy Hansen; pp. 92–93, Ivy Hansen; p. 96, Ivy Hansen; p. 100, Ivy Hansen; p. 109, Ivy Hansen; pp. 112–3, Ivy Hansen; p. 116, Bay Picture Library; p. 117, Bay Picture Library; p. 120, Ivy Hansen; p. 121, John Squire (b l); p. 121, Bay Picture Library (b r); p. 124, Ivy Hansen (t l); p. 124, Bay Picture Library (b l); p. 125, Bay Picture Library; p. 129, Bay Picture Library; p. 131, Bay Picture Library; p. 132, Ivy Hansen (b l); p. 132, John Squire (b r); p. 133, Bay Picture Library; p. 136, Bay Picture Library; p. 137, John Squire; p. 138, Bay Picture Library; p. 141, John Squire (t l); p. 141, Bay Picture Library (b r); p. 144, John Squire; p. 145, John Squire; p. 148, Bay Picture Library; p. 149, Ivy Hansen; p. 152, John Squire; p. 153, Bay Picture Library; p. 156, John Squire (t l); p. 156, Ivy Hansen (t r); p. 157, Bay Picture Library; p. 161, Bay Picture Library; p. 163, Bay Picture Library; p. 164, Ivy Hansen; p. 165, Sporting Pix; p. 168, Bay Picture Library; back cover, Ivy Hansen.

ILLUSTRATIONS

Illustrations are in page order. Unless otherwise stated, all illustrations © Angus&Robertson.
In all other cases, copyright remains with the individual illustrator.

Page 8, Sarah Forshaw; p. 9, Sarah Forshaw; p. 101, Sarah Forshaw.

BLACK AND WHITE PRINTS

All black and white prints are reproductions of Victorian prints.

PHOTO CAPTIONS

Front cover: *Blechnum wattsii.*
Page i: *Gleichenia dicarpa.*
Page iv: *Platycerium hillii* (t l).
Pages iv–v: *Blechnum brasiliense.*
Page 1: *Todites pattinsoniorum* fossil from the Triassic period, about 220 million years old.
Pages 12–13: Dried ferns from a Victorian fern album.
Pages 32–33: *Asplenium nidus.*
Pages 56–57: *Selaginella willldenovii.*
Pages 64–65: *Asplenium bulbiferum.*
Pages 76–77: *Dicksonia antarctica.*
Pages 92–93: *Adiantum raddianum fragrans.*
Pages: 112–3: *Microsorium scandens.*
Back cover: *Asplenium nidus.*